8/10

Schmitt

GROWING STUFF

AN ALTERNATIVE
GUIDE TO GARDENING

black dog publishing
london uk

CONTENTS

GROWING STUFF
AN ALTERNATIVE GUIDE TO GARDENING

FOREWORD

RICHARD REYNOLDS

The inspiration for growing stuff comes from all around us. Summer evenings in a friend's back garden, the nose-twitching array of a florist's stall, a flowerpot-packed windowsill spotted from the top deck of a bus, the childhood memory of mucking around outdoors, the incredible taste of someone's home-grown produce and the greener grass on the other side of your fence.

For me, weeds are a great source of inspiration. Without us doing anything (except perhaps sitting back and letting the patio crumble), seeds sprout, plants bloom and our neighbourhoods gradually get greener. On the tiniest ledge, in shadowy alleyways, in the bleakest of concrete courtyards, weeds show us that plants will grow almost anywhere; they are green clues to the potential in our gardens and within the landscape all around us.

But though you may admire the dandelions and young butterfly bushes bursting forth, do not fall for the charm of their independent and self-sufficient nature! They have their own agenda—and it's not necessarily the same as yours. The beauty, fragrance and deliciousness that we love about plants are of course incidental to their main mission—to reproduce—and weeds do this best. Left entirely to their own devices the most pioneering of plants can become Triffid-like creatures that seem to gobble up all in their path. So don't sit back: instead take a leaf from the book of weeds, spot the potential out there and grow stuff you want. Plants appreciate some help anyway, as not all have the stamina to thrive without you playing a part in their life. With a little nurturing encouragement using the advice and inspiration in the pages of this book you will be growing stuff in no time.

With weeds (and, quite often, a colourful bed of litter) as my starting point I have managed to grow plants in thoroughly unpromising circumstances. As a guerrilla gardener I have transformed neglected public land in my neighbourhood regardless of the horticultural and bureaucratic obstacles. Eager to grow stuff, and without a patch of my own, I spotted opportunity in these local spaces. The resulting gardens are far more beautiful (and sometimes tastier too) than the orphaned land had become. Seeing plants flourish in the middle of swirling traffic and unremarkable urban scrub become a productive garden has been the most satisfying gardening I've done. The triumph of growing plants in seemingly inhospitable environments is immense (although had some windowsills, a balcony or even the luxury of a garden been available to me I'd have certainly started there first!).

Growing stuff is a joyful double act between you and the plant—usually with the plant providing the most laughs. A favourite, the giant sunflower, with a bit of help, gives a pedestrian-stopping performance during its short but glorious life. I'm proud to see it tower radiantly next to a bus stop, smiling down at passersby. I did my bit sparing the seed from an early death-by-salad, deciding where it would grow, rescuing it from slugs in its tender early weeks and propping it up with a supporting bamboo cane in old age. After barely six months the sunflower will have died but it will in turn give up a useful harvest in its huge head of seed. That is the time to make that salad or seed-encrusted loaf of bread, with plenty left over to sow next spring. A plant's success is your success too.

More of us are growing stuff these days, but just think what cities would look like if we were all gardeners, making use of the bountiful opportunities within private gardens, rooftops and beyond our private boundaries. We could have garden cities—which itself is not a new idea. Just over 100 years ago the Englishman Ebenezer Howard wrote about his vision of 'garden cities'. The solution he proposed to the congested, polluted and rather debilitating life in cities during the late nineteenth century was to start from scratch and build new towns in new places. These would have homes with large private gardens, and wide cultivated boulevards with easy access to allotments and farmland. The garden city was to combine the best of the countryside with the best of the city, with stuff growing all over the place. Howard's conception of garden cities soon became a movement, with some even being built during the first half of the last century. But the sprawling space needed for such verdant communities and lush suburbs revealed itself to be not entirely practical, and there still remained the issue of what to do about the older, densely populated urban spaces of previous generations—knocking down great swathes of them and rebuilding is rather wasteful, (although it was popular for a while)! So today, the garden city solution is different. It's not about moving home but moving mindset—it's about adapting your gardens and communities and growing stuff. If we don't, the weeds will.

GETTING STARTED

GROWING STUFF
AN ALTERNATIVE GUIDE TO GARDENING

INTRODUCTION
ELIZABETH MCCORQUODALE

Growing stuff is engagingly, fundamentally, intensely satisfying. Whether the stuff you grow consists of a couple of pots of sprouting seeds on a sunny windowsill, a balcony overflowing with baskets of herbs and flowers or a garden space dedicated to the production of prize blooms and veg, the sense of satisfaction is undeniable. And if you sit down one day and eat the stuff you've grown, especially if you've started it off from scratch yourself, that satisfaction is increased tenfold.

Whether your garden becomes an occasional pleasure or an obsession depends on how much time you want to put into it and how much space you have. One thing is certain—anybody, anywhere, can grow stuff. To get started you need only the smallest amount of know-how and the most basic of equipment: something to grow and somewhere to put it, and not much more.

You can assemble all the ingredients needed for your venture completely free of charge. Enthusiasts will fall over themselves to convert you, offering you cuttings and seedlings and small screws of paper containing the last of the previous year's seed. It is nothing but a compliment to suggest to another gardener that the next time they lift a clump of mint (or rhubarb or artichokes...) whether they would mind putting a little piece aside for you. After all, you are just confirming their knowledge that the plants they grow are worth sharing.

Pots for sowing seeds, for making a display of herbs or growing a crop of potatoes are all free and freely available, if you want them to be. Even the soil you grow them in can be free and made by you.

More and more people are becoming involved in 'growing their own', whether that means a square-foot garden of summer vegetables, an entire allotment or a blueberry bush in an old pot. The media abounds with pieces that reflect the growing interest in becoming—at least a little bit—self-sufficient. Those novelties and necessities which have tempted people away from looking after themselves are showing themselves to be tainted—by the use of chemicals, the over-exploitation of natural resources and the unethical use of 'unskilled' labour here and abroad. The leisure generation has to work harder and harder to be able to afford their easy life and the apparent convenience and speed of 'modern' living is, perhaps, too much of a compromise. We want to know what we're eating and where it comes from and we've found that growing some of it ourselves can be, in turns, therapeutic, absorbing, and more than a little fun.

TOP TOOLS

SPADES AND FORKS

You will need a spade if you are going to do any sort of digging in the ground. Choose a size and weight that is comfortable; for example, a large, long-handled steel spade would make any digging extremely hard work for a small, slight person. The join between the handle and blade should be high up the handle, for strength, and the edge of the blade should be sharp to slice through soil and roots.

Forks are used for breaking up heavy soil and digging up root crops like potatoes and carrots. All the same things apply for forks as they do for spades in terms of size, weight and strength. At a pinch you could get away with one or the other—it largely depends on how much time you will spend using them—but they each do their own job very well. Always, always bring your garden fork and spade inside when you have finished and store them in a dry place to prevent the handles rotting.

If your gardening is to be done in pots (or recycled bags or an old sink) you need only the most basic of equipment; something to hold water and deliver it to your plants, something to scoop the soil, and perhaps a means by which you can provide support for your growing plants. You may also need scissors or secateurs, string or twine and plant labels.

If you have the space, the time and the inclination to grow stuff in an allotment or in your own garden (or your neighbour's!) you will need more in the way of equipment; a digging spade and a garden fork as a minimum, and probably a hoe and a wheelbarrow as well.

There is no maximum to the time, effort and money you can invest in growing stuff, but there is, thankfully, a very small and adequate minimum.

TROWELS

To fill seed trays and small pots with soil you can make a perfect scoop from a plastic milk bottle by cutting away the side (see illustration). Alternatively use a sturdy plastic plant pot to scoop up the soil, or opt for a trowel. Trowels should be comfortable to hold and be very sturdy, especially at the shank where the handle joins the metal; if it bends, don't buy it. A sturdy trowel is a necessity if you garden in the ground or in raised beds.

SECATEURS AND SCISSORS

Secateurs or 'snips' are used for cleanly cutting through anything up to about 1 cm in diameter that ordinary kitchen scissors can't cut. Professional gardeners become obsessively attached to their secateurs and that's simply because they, more than any other tool, become an extension of yourself when you use them. There are many types of secateurs, and different people sing the praises of the various kinds—the general rules are try them out, buy the best you can, and keep them sharp.

WATERING CANS

If you only have a small balcony or windowsill on which to do your growing, you don't need anything but a jug from the kitchen and an old plastic drinks bottle complete with its lid. Poke holes into the lid with a heated metal skewer or a hammer and nail and use the bottle to water your seeds and seedlings. The spray is exactly right and you have more control over where the water ends up than if you were to use a small watering can with a rose.

With more plants to water, whether they are in pots or a garden, you'll need a bucket, and a jug or a conventional watering can. Choose one that fits under your tap easily and, for the bigger cans, one that has a handle at the top as well as at the rear. The rose, the attachment at the end of the spout that allows the water to sprinkle rather than gush, needs to be detachable so that you can dislodge any debris (like the inevitable troglodyte snail) that becomes stuck in the spout.

HOES

You will only need to add this to your arsenal if you have a conventional patch of garden—intensive 'square foot' gardening, where plants are crammed in tightly in small spaces, and container gardening, need the close attention of a gloved hand instead.

Hoes are used to slice the tops off weeds, usually between rows of vegetables. The weeds are then gathered up and composted or, if there are a lot of seeding weeds, burnt. Using a hoe is a very quick and efficient way of dealing with the inevitable jungle of weeds that grow whenever your back is turned. Look out for a long handle and a sharp blade; modern hoes don't have long handles so picking one up second-hand is a wise move.

SEED TRAYS AND SMALL POTS

Seeds and seedlings can be started off in conventional seed trays or just as easily in old yoghurt pots, plastic fruit punnets, the tubes from toilet or kitchen rolls or the disposable cup that held your morning coffee. The list of alternative seed trays is vast. Whatever you use, remember to clean it thoroughly first and to poke a few holes in the bottom. And once you have sown your seed, label it!

LABELS

There are few things so frustrating as a table full of newly planted pots and trays and no clue as to which pot holds which seed! Make it a habit to label things as you go along. The little plastic plant labels that are sold in garden centres are fine but just as practical—and a lot less expensive—is an indelible marker and a plastic milk bottle. Cut the bottle into strips about 2.5 cm wide by 10 cm long, write the full name of the seed and the date of planting on your label and pop it into the side of your pot.

GOING POTTY

Take one old wellie boot, add soil, seeds and a sprinkling of water and, magically, you have a garden. Containers can come in all shapes and sizes and reflect all manner of delightful eccentricities, from an old tin trunk, a recycled washing machine drum to a capacious old handbag. A pair of old and shabby work boots sporting a top-knot of strawberries can become the perfect pot to adorn the front steps of your house.

There are no rules when it comes to choosing or adapting a found object to hold your plants. The challenge, then, may be to come up with something quite unique.

TRY THESE MAKESHIFT CONTAINERS

Wellie boots and work boots
An old chest of drawers, each drawer pulled out and planted in a cascade
Old laundry basket
Car tyres and car wheels
Holey old water butt
Saucepans and teapots
Old handbags and suitcases
Old zinc buckets, baths and churns
Porcelain sinks and baths
Hanging baskets

JUST A BIT OF OLD DIRT

Soil or potting compost has to do several things; anchor the plant, hold on to and supply nutrients, retain water and allow water to drain away. It is a lot to ask from a bit of old dirt. How do you choose from among the huge number on sale?

POTTING COMPOST

The quick answer for the true beginner is to find a supplier, locally or via the internet, who sells certified organic, peat-free, multi-purpose compost by the bag.

If, however, you have already started the process of turning your kitchen scraps into soil via a compost bin or a wormery, then you are at least halfway to producing your own potting compost. There are as many recipes for home-made potting soils as there are for home-made chocolate chip cookies—just opt for using what you have at hand while keeping in mind that the purpose is to retain enough moisture without becoming waterlogged. If you get the consistency right you can deal with the nutrients later.

Compost is precious stuff, so eke it out a little with clean (weed and seed-free) crumbly garden soil dug from your own or a friend's garden, and something to increase the drainage in the form of sand or grit.

If you stick to roughly three parts compost from your bin, two parts clean garden soil and one part sand or grit, you won't go far wrong.

Every type of garden soil, from sandy to stony, will benefit from the addition of as much composted kitchen and garden waste as you can throw at it.

SEED COMPOST

Seedlings hate to get soggy. Compost used for growing seeds is simply ordinary potting soil with something added to help with drainage.

For the small-scale grower it makes most sense to take a little of the soil you will grow your mature plants in, and add a quantity of sand—maybe from a children's sand pit—or fine grit at a quantity of three parts potting compost to one part sand.

GARDEN SOIL

Garden soil needs to provide a nutritious, comfortable bed for your plants and one that will allow roots to grow down into it. The only way to prepare your new soil for planting is to dig it through and break it up. If you have clay or stony soil this can be really hard work but you will reap the benefits in healthier, happier plants and enormously increased yields. If the soil structure is really appalling and you have access to a large supply of good compost or farm manure you have the option of building raised beds. These are simply wooden frames laid on top of your existing soil and filled with compost or topsoil brought in from elsewhere. Old pallets can be dismantled to provide the sides and you can build them as long as you want, provided you restrict the width to a manageable 1.2 metres. Failing that, add as much compost as you can and keep on digging!

THE ACQUISITIVE GARDENER
WHERE TO GET PLANTS

It would seem that the most obvious place to go for your new plants and seeds would be to your local garden centre. However, this isn't the most prudent option either for your purse or your planet. Gardening is very big business and vast amounts of time and money are spent by the industry in marketing their products in a way that will encourage us to buy things on a whim.

SMALL IS BEAUTIFUL

Independent nurseries, whether local affairs raising and selling annual flowers and vegetable plants, or specialist outfits concentrating on one type of exotic plant, usually have the advantage that the owners have a real enthusiasm for their plants. You can find some real treasures as well as sound advice at many nurseries.

GETTING THE MOST FROM GARDEN CENTRES

Standing in front of a seed display containing hundreds of varieties of seeds can be both terribly tempting and confusing in the extreme—a recipe for disappointment. Before you go, arm yourself with a seed catalogue (available over the internet) and spend some time deciding what you want. Take a look around at the various seed producers; many produce a kids' seed range retailing at a fraction of the price of the top-drawer lines. There may be fewer seeds per packet but it's an economical way to buy some varieties such as sunflowers, nasturtiums, cress and lettuce.

Seeds are sold off cheaply at the end of summer, and they remain viable long after the following spring.

Make the bargain corner your first stop for plants. Most, as long as they're not diseased or infested, will make a quick recovery when given a good home. Plants are usually sold according to pot size so look for large plants in small pots to get value for money. It isn't unusual to get several plants from one pot if you know what to look for. Lots of herbs and perennial flowers and some fruit can be tipped out of their pot and gently teased apart to make many

smaller plants; mint, marjoram, creeping thymes, dill, chives and strawberries are among them. Potted up, these smaller plants will grow away happily to give you more plants for your money to either use or swap.

SWAPPING WITH FRIENDS

If you grow too many plants you may have enough to exchange with friends or neighbours. Having an abundance of unwanted plants gives you currency to open trade negotiations and even if your trading partners are short on desirable items at the time, it's money in the bank as far as you're concerned when it comes to next season's swaps.

You could take advantage of the often very large numbers of seeds in each packet and arrange a seed-sharing scheme with friends or neighbours. Decide what you each want to grow, share the expense and share out the seed, or decide that each member of the group will raise a particular variety of plant so that the swap takes place at the plant stage instead.

OFFICIAL SWAP SHOPS

Look in your local press, in gardening magazines and on the internet for times and venues of official Seedy Sundays and other swap shops. These can be places to swap seeds, seed potatoes and plants, and although there is sometimes a nominal fee, entrance is often free. On the day, take along your surplus seeds, packaged and labelled and exchange them at the door for a token or ticket for you to use as currency. Besides the stalls that offer the donated seed, carefully sorted and arranged appropriately for you to choose from, there is often a scattering of other stalls giving advice or selling their horticultural wares.

RECYCLING WEBSITES

Websites like Freecycle are usually run to serve a local community, and are a wonderful boon to anyone who grows anything. As well as posting your unwanted seeds, plants or pots, and perusing the offered items, you can also post a plea for a vital plant or piece of equipment. Among the gardening items that appear most often are seed potatoes, raspberry canes, spare pots, old baths for planting or pond life, and plants of all kinds. Just don't forget to give as well as receive!

YOUR LOCAL PAPER

In these you can often find gardening treasures of all kinds, including tools, and you can return the favour sometime with your own offering of produce or plants.

SCHOOL AND COMMUNITY FAIRS AND FETES

Lot of lovely and often interesting varieties of plants are offered at very reasonable prices at these events, with the added bonus that your money is going to a good cause. If you're serious about your plant-hunting make sure you're there at the beginning of the day—otherwise wander along later when the real bargains are on offer.

GROWING, GROWING, GROWN!

THE 1, 2, 3 OF SOWING SEEDS

1. Choose your container. If you have the space it is always best to start seeds off in individual containers so that their roots don't have to be disturbed at a later date.

2. Fill your chosen container with potting soil to 5 mm below the rim so that you can water easily without water and seeds spilling over the edge. Firm the soil down gently.

3. Sow your seed to the correct depth (see table), one or two per individual pot or very thinly in a seed tray such as an old strawberry punnet. Imagine for a moment the time when they all spring to life—will each of your tiny seedlings have the space to grow several leaves and a healthy little clump of roots without becoming entangled with their neighbours?

4. Pop a small polythene bag over your pot and hold it away from the compost with the help of a wooden skewer or thin cane pushed carefully into the soil. This little transparent tepee will conserve moisture while letting the condensation that gathers inside the bag roll away harmlessly.

5. Place your pots on a bright, but not sun-baked, windowsill. Full sunlight at this stage may reduce a tiny seedling to nothing in no time at all and too little light will mean leggy, weak growth. Ensure the spot you choose is warm, even at night time, and free of draughts.

6. Water carefully. Don't let the soil become too wet or too dry. Only observation can govern when or how much to water.

7. Watch your seedlings appear. Exactly when this will happen depends on what you're growing. As soon as their little seed leaves appear fully above the soil remove and recycle the polythene covering. It is at this stage that seedlings are at their most vulnerable, but a good balance of moisture and air circulation will do the trick.

SOWING DEPTHS FOR SEED

5 mm deep
Tiny seeds such as tomato, peppers, celery and lettuce.

1.25 cm deep
Medium seeds such as carrot, radish, beets, cabbage, broccoli, cauliflower, leeks, spinach and swede.

3.5 cm deep
Large seeds such as corn, cucumber, pumpkin, squash, melon, onion, courgettes, beans and peas.

SOWING SEEDS: TIPS

Some plants are easy to start from seed and some are more demanding. Knowing the tricks and truths of planting and raising seeds will ensure you a trouble-free journey into the world of micro-propagation.

- Sow seed at the correct depth in the soil according to its size (see table).

- Sow cucurbit seeds (marrow, melon, squash, cucumber) and other flat seeds on their sides.

- Do not exclude light, as many seeds need light to germinate.

- Remove the cover from your seed tray as soon as the majority of tiny seedlings in that container have appeared.

- The fewer times you disturb the roots of your new plants the happier they will be and the quicker they will grow.

- Seedlings hate being soggy.

- Be ruthless with poorly or overcrowded plants. It's much better to pinch out (cut off at soil level) one of a pair of healthy seedlings now, than distress both of them later by pulling them apart.

- Handle seedlings and young plants by their leaves, never by their stems, to avoid damaging them.

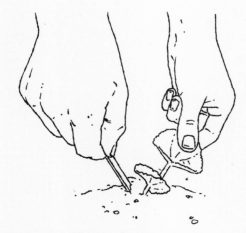

FROM SEEDLINGS TO PLANTS

If you have started your seeds off in trays rather than individual pots you will need to transplant or 'prick out' your seedlings into individual pots to give them more room to grow. When your seedlings are large enough to handle and have at least two sets of true leaves, prepare enough 8 cm pots for all your plants by filling them with ordinary potting compost to within 5 mm of the rim and make a hole in the soil to accommodate the seedling.

With the tip of a pencil or a lolly stick, loosen the soil gently beneath one seedling and, holding it carefully by a leaf, use the lolly stick to lift it up and into its new bed. Plant it so that the junction between soil and stem is at exactly the same level as it was in the seed tray. Firm it in very gently, water carefully with tepid water and finally, label it.

Continue until you have planted all your seedlings. It's at this stage that you will probably realise just how many plants you have to trade with friends!

If you have started your seeds off in individual pots from the beginning you can bypass this stage altogether.

MOVING PLANTS TO THEIR PERMANENT HOME

When your plants begin to put on strong, new growth and roots begin to appear in the holes in the bottom of their pots, it's time to move them to their final home. Acclimatise those plants that are set to live outside by putting them out during the day and bringing them inside at night. Continue to do this until all risk of frost has passed in your area. The general guide for the UK is about the middle of May, bearing in mind that some plants are very tender indeed, while others are hardier souls and can tolerate quite a lot of cold weather.

Begin to prepare large containers by putting in something that will prevent the very bottom of the pots becoming a soggy mess—a layer of broken pots or tiles, stones or bits of polystyrene packaging will do. Fill the container with potting compost to within 2.5–5 cm of the rim, depending on the size of your container. Smaller permanent containers and hanging baskets need all their space filled with potting compost and will also benefit from the addition of a water-absorbing substance. This can be the crystals that are available from every garden centre or the eco alternative based on kelp seaweed which is available through organic garden suppliers.

Transfer your plants into their new home without handling the stem, plant at the same depth as they are accustomed, and water thoroughly.

TAKING CUTTINGS

You can get new plants from old ones by taking a piece of stem or small branch and encouraging it to grow new roots. Taking stem cuttings is easy and, for some plants such as rosemary and lavender, is the quickest way to get new plants without buying them. Which kind of cutting you take depends on the plant you are increasing. You can choose to use rooting powder, a substance that contains plant hormones to encourage root growth, however most softwood cuttings will happily root without. For the slower growth of hardwood cuttings there are organic rooting powders available.

SOFTWOOD CUTTINGS

These are taken from the soft, green stems of plants such as mint, thyme, lemon balm, lavender and rosemary and other perennial plants that don't have or haven't developed a woody stem.

1. Cut a healthy-looking stem about 10 cm long from the top of your chosen plant.

2. Strip the leaves from the lower half of the stem and, if using, dust the cut with rooting powder.

3. Push the cutting one third of the way into a pot of sand mixed with a little compost and loosely cover the pot and cutting with a polythene bag. Use a wooden skewer pushed into the sand to prevent the bag from touching your cutting.

4. Place the pot out of direct sunlight and wait for roots and new top growth to appear. Mint will root in two or three weeks but other plants can take up to three months to root.

SEMI-HARDWOOD CUTTINGS

As the name suggests, these are taken from plants that have developed a woodier stem. This type of cutting will take longer to root but the thrill of growing something as sturdy and permanent as a blueberry or blackcurrant bush from scratch is hard to beat. Other plants that will propagate in this method are bay, red and white currants and gooseberries, older rosemary stems, and sage, as well as many flowering shrubs.

1. Take a cutting about 10–15 cm long with a diameter no bigger than a slim pencil. Make your cut diagonally, just below a leaf node (the swelling where a leaf arises from a stem or branch). The diagonal cut exposes more of the root-producing area of the stem.

2. Repeat steps 2–4 as described opposite. For instructional diagrams, see page 79.

LAYERING

This is really just nature's way of taking cuttings for you. The stems of many herbs and perennial fruit and vegetables will root if they are in contact with the ground. Probably the best known for doing this are strawberries, but rosemary, mint, sage, southernwood, currants and gooseberries will do the same. All you need to do is choose a stem and bend it gently to the ground. Help your new plant on its way by loosening the soil at the point of contact and peg the stem to the ground with a stone or a loop made from a wire coat hanger. In late spring, when growth is quick, roots may develop in as little as two weeks; at other times it may take the whole summer before roots appear. When a good clump of roots is apparent and your shoot is growing happily you can cut the ties to the parent plant and move your plant to its new home.

TOMATO BASICS

THREE BASICS OF TOMATO SELECTION

OUTDOOR OR GREENHOUSE
This is determined by how weather-resistant and quick-growing the tomato plants are.

BUSH AND CORDON
Bush tomatoes are also known as 'determinate', and cordon varieties also known as 'indeterminate'.

Bush tomatoes are exactly that—shorter (they grow to a maximum of about 75 cm)—and they require no pruning or pinching. This group includes the type that can be grown in hanging baskets.

Cordons are taller and grown as a single stem, straight up a support such as a string or cane.

TYPE OF FRUIT
The last delicious choice to make is what type of fruit you want: tiny or gigantic, red, orange, yellow or striped, sweet or tangy; there are literally hundreds to choose from.

You can have any combination of the three basics; for example, you can have tiny plum tomatoes growing in hanging baskets outside, or up a 3 metre cane in a greenhouse. The name and variety will of course be different, as will the care they need from you.

TOMATO TIPS

If you only want a few tomato plants you can sow your seed two per pot, directly into small, 8 cm pots of compost. But be ruthless and pinch out the weaker of the two seedlings when your tomatoes are about 5 cm tall.

Tomatoes will repay every extra bit of sunshine, warmth, regular feeding and watering with bigger, tastier yields.

Gardeners of old used to put hair trimmings and wood ash in the base of their tomato pots before planting, both of which are excellent sources of slowly released potassium, an essential nutrient for a good tomato crop.

PRUNING TOMATOES

All side shoots (branches) growing from the leaf axils (where leaves join onto the stem) are cut off when they are 2.5 cm long. There is no danger of cutting off a potential fruiting stem (truss), as these don't grow from the same place. If you have a greenhouse or very sheltered and protected spot you can leave your cordons to grow to about 1.8 metres tall (or even taller in a heated greenhouse)—otherwise pinch out the tops when the plant is about four feet tall. This will stop your plant growing upwards and allow it to put all its energy into ripening existing fruit rather than putting out new green growth.

FERTILISER AND FEED

Plants need a supply of the main nutrients: nitrogen for healthy green leaves, phosphorus for strong root growth and potassium (potash) for the development of fruit and flowers, as well as smaller quantities of micronutrients. If they are grown in good quality compost made from a variety of materials there should be little trouble in supplying everything that is needed for healthy growth. However at some stages, like when the plant is heavy with fruit, extra nutrients are needed.

The very best stuff to use is homemade, organic feed, of which there are many types. Easy to make and free into the bargain, home brewed feed can be adapted to specifically encourage the production of roots, leaves, fruit and flowers. Liquid feed made from the 'juice' drained from the bottom of a wormery or from nettles or comfrey soaked in water make great all-round fertilisers —see page 106.

Eggshells (calcium), seaweed and wood ash (potash) can all be added to your compost heap or liquid feed brew to increase the goodness and give a nutrient boost.

Organic and natural fertilisers formulated for specific purposes are available in the shops, particularly liquid seaweed feed and chicken manure pellets, both of which are suitable.

MUCK, GLORIOUS MUCK

Grab yourself a bucket or two and head along to the local stables. But remember that what goes in must come out and if the horses in the stable are fed on a diet heavy in supplements and additives, then some of that will end up in their muck. Make enquiries about their feeding regime and cross your fingers. There really is nothing so good as well rotted manure to give plants a boost; add it to your compost heap or put it on the ground in the autumn and just watch your plants romp away.

PRUNING AND DEADHEADING

Although not completely essential, pruning is a useful technique that helps tame plants and keep them in shape, and allows for better and more abundant growth. It's not as complex as you might think; all you need to do is remove older branches to make way for new growth and brighter flowers. Pruning is important for removing dead growth and diseased stems should be removed to prevent spread. Plants can be pruned quite vigorously as this will allow the plant to put its energy into putting out new shoots. Deadheading has an obvious aesthetic purpose, allowing you to clear away dead flowers and maintain the beauty of your plant. It can also prolong bloom time, increase flower yield and even stimulate a second bloom.

For plants that flower and fruit in spring and early summer, prune as soon as they fade, in late summer or autumn. These plants bloom on new growth each year, so this will allow the plant time to regrow with fresh shoots.

Plants that flower or friut in late summer tend to bloom on the current year's growth—prune these in late winter or early spring.

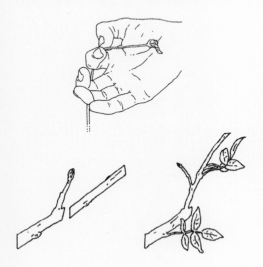

1. As a general rule, try to leave enough of a branch to allow regrowth. It is best to cut back to just above a bud or new branch.

2. For shrubs such as rosemary and woody plants, remove dead, diseased, or dying branches, and any straggly branches. This will help keep the plant in shape and encourage bushy, full growth.

3. On flowering bedding and container plants, pinch or cut out any fading flowers or flower stalks. This will stimulate the production of new flowers, as the plant will otherwise expend its energy on producing seeds for germination.

4. Put any plant matter you remove on the compost heap—unless it is diseased.

5. Don't prune during extreme weather—either too hot or too cold —as this can harm your plant.

6. Keep secateurs sharp, as blunt blades can damage branches.

7. To prune lavender you need to cut out damaged branches and keep it trim by cutting only into new growth—you can't 'renovate' a leggy, overgrown lavender bush; instead, take softwood cuttings from it and grow new ones.

GOLDEN RULES OF PRUNING

Always think before you cut.

You can't stick it back on again.

Never give a plant a haircut (an all-over trim of the tops of all the branches) as this will result in a witch's broom effect.

You can prune most established plants by cutting out about a third of the total growth, taking the oldest branches down to just above ground level after flowering or fruiting.

COMPOSTING
TRINA TUNE

Composting is great for the environment and your garden. It cuts down household waste, reduces greenhouse gas emissions and improves soil organically. Best of all, composting systems can be cheap to set up, easy to run and fit almost anywhere. There are a variety of composting methods and ways to contain your organic matter—from a simple heap, pit or enclosure to bins, barrels and worm farms. All have their advantages and varying reasons for use.

Food and garden waste in landfill produces methane gas, which as a greenhouse gas is 21 times more potent than carbon dioxide. By reducing the need for transporting such waste, fewer fossil fuels are burned, which means fewer greenhouse gases and pollutants in the air. Sending organic rubbish to landfill is also a waste of good composting material, which is essential in building good, healthy soil.

While composting is great for households with a backyard and room for a compost bin or heap, worm farms are ideal for smaller places. Worm farms are excellent for small areas like balconies and courtyards because they are compact and relatively tidy. Worm castings (excrement) and juice (liquid runoff) make excellent organic soil conditioner and fertiliser for both bedding and potted plants. See page 104 for how to build your own worm farm.

SETTING UP A COMPOST SYSTEM

Whether you use a bin or just a simple heap, compost systems ideally need to be set up on a sunny, well drained spot that receives some shade in summer. Although compost decomposes faster if it is hot, it is important that it doesn't dry out.

Add about a spade full of compost from a previous batch or some garden soil to help introduce good microorganisms into the heap. If you are using a bin, ensure you line the base with wire mesh to keep rats and mice from burrowing into the organic material. Another vermin deterrent is burying the bin a few centimetres into the soil or building some soil up around the edges of the bin.

Add a layer of sticks or large prunings to the bottom of the heap to help create space for air circulation.

Compost needs to be kept moist, like a damp sponge. Cover the top of the heap with something that will preserve moisture—an old carpet or some plastic sheeting is ideal. If you are using a bin, ensure its lid has small holes to let rain and air through.

WHAT TO ADD TO COMPOST

The more different varieties of organic matter added to a compost, the richer it will be. Almost all organic matter can be added to a compost bin; however, if you are just starting out with composting steer clear of meat, fish, dairy and fats because they attract vermin.

A good mixture of elements for a compost is about 20 parts carbon to one part nitrogen. High carbon, or 'brown' ingredients are: dry leaves, twiggy prunings, sawdust, paper, straw, dry grass, wood ash (not coal), shredded paper and ripped up cardboard.

Ingredients high in nitrogen, or 'green' ingredients are vegetable and fruit scraps, fresh lawn clippings, farm animal manure (no pet droppings), old vase flowers, garden clippings, coffee grounds, tea leaves and seaweed. However, before taking seaweed from a beach get permission from the local council first.

Other wastes that can be composted are hair, fluff, vacuum cleaner dust, used potting mix, crushed egg shells and old clothes.

WHAT NOT TO ADD TO COMPOST

Although some compost systems can get quite hot, they rarely get to temperatures that can properly kill off weed seeds and diseases. To ensure you don't spread such nasties, keep weed seeds and disease-infected plants out of the heap.

If you do want to add them, kill off the seeds and diseases first by placing them in a sealed clear plastic bag in the sun for a few months before adding them to the heap.

Fruit fly infested fruit should also be boiled or sealed in a plastic bag and stored in the sun for at least a week before composting. Don't add large amounts of salty water because salt is no good for soil or plants. Large woody prunings also take too long to break down and excrement from humans and meat-eating pets (dogs and cats) is not recommended because it may contain harmful bacteria or intestinal worm larvae. However, it is possible to compost the bedding from vegetarian pets like rabbits and guinea pigs.

IMPROVING AERATION

Turning the compost frequently is essential for getting good aeration into the mix and helping it heat up. This can be done with a shovel, garden fork or compost corkscrew. You can also insert a piece of plastic agricultural pipe with slits or holes into the centre of the heap to help bring air into the organic material.

If your bin is a closed plastic bin, drill small holes in the side to improve aeration. Use fly screen (available from camping shops) on the inside of the bin to cover the holes and prevent flies from entering.

Compost worms will also help turn your compost and aerate it. Some ingredients that help activate the heat in compost are fresh grass clippings, comfrey, farm manure, urine and seaweed.

COMPOSTING METHODS

LAYERING

This technique is good if you plan to constantly add organic matter to the system. Add alternate layers of green and brown materials and try to add a thin layer of soil and a handful of fertiliser such as blood and bone on top of each layer. The heap will continue to shrink, allowing more space for extra organic matter.

ALL IN TOGETHER

This method is good if you have all of your ingredients ready. Combine kitchen and garden waste, plus fertiliser at the same time. Turn several times a week to generate a lot of heat to break down the pile quickly. Tumbler style compost bins are ideal for this method of composting because the tumbler method makes it easy to turn the bin regularly.

WHEN IS COMPOST READY?

A good compost can break down within about four to ten weeks but it does depend on many different variables such as climate, ingredients and care.

Compost is ready when there are no recognisable pieces of the original organic material. The organic waste will be converted to a dark brown, crumbly, sweet smelling earth-like substance that should contain plenty of worms. Add compost to your garden or pot plant soil, or use it as mulch on the soil's surface. To avoid fungal decay don't pile compost up against tree trunks or plant stems.

TROUBLE-SHOOTING

Although composting is relatively easy, there are a few things that can go wrong.

A smelly compost can mean it is too wet or not getting enough air. Fork in dry leaves, shredded paper or garden mulch and make sure you turn the heap regularly to increase air circulation. A common cause can also be too many food scraps and not enough dry ingredients. Too many nitrogen-rich ingredients will cause the heap to get acidic. To reduce acidity add garden lime, dolomite or woodfire ash.

If your organic matter doesn't seem to be decomposing fast enough it could be because it is not hot enough or it is not getting enough air or water. To fix this problem add more nitrogen-rich material such as kitchen or green garden organics to speed up the composting process. Turn the heap and add water. If the heap gets too cold in winter, try covering it with an insulating material.

COMMON TYPES OF COMPOST SYSTEMS

COMPOST BINS

Compost bins come in a variety of shapes and sizes. They are usually made from recycled or new plastic, and bottomless. It can be difficult to turn the material in the bin—using a garden fork or compost corkscrew can help; lifting the bin off the heap and turning the compost can also work.

COMPOST BARRELS

These are generally cylindrical plastic or metal bins that rotate on a frame. The drum opens at the end or on the side and contains air vents for oxygen circulation. They either rotate on their sides or are turned upside down to aerate the compost. Providing the bin is not too full and heavy, it can be quite easy to turn and is a better option for people who physically struggle to turn compost.

ENCLOSURES

Enclosures can be made from any simple structure, like timber, chicken wire, bales of hay or railway sleepers to enclose the compost heap. This method is very low-tech and cheap to produce; however, it is not very vermin proof or portable.

COMPOST HEAPS

These are very low-tech, economical and easy to build. Heaps require nothing more than roughly one square metre of space on soil, preferably in a sunny spot. Again, not vermin-proof or portable and a little messy for the tidy-conscious.

PITS OR TRENCHES

This is probably the simplest method of composting because you just need to dig a hole and place the organic matter into it. Cover the hole with soil and the organic matter will eventually break down.

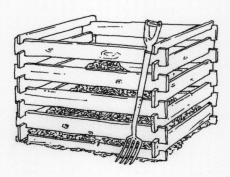

GUIDE TO PEST CONTROL

There is no doubt that as you garden, you'll come across some unwanted creepy crawlies. However, it is important to consider whether you really need to remove these from your garden, or whether you can try humane ways to control their populations. There are ways to keep pests under control that can help balance, rather than damage, the local ecosystem. Try some of the following organic suggestions.

CONTROLLING INSECT POPULATION

Wherever possible, avoid chemical pesticides and slug pellets. Although they might help clear your garden of slugs and snails, they're also poisonous to the birds, frogs and hedgehogs that feed on them.

Cover delicate seedlings overnight with an upturned plastic punnet, to protect them.

A favourite slug-ridding technique is to place bowls or yoghurt pots filled with beer or milk around your garden. Position them so that the rim of the dish is level with the soil—slugs are attracted by the scent which is to them reminiscent or rotting fruit, and they will drown in the alcohol.

Simply go round your garden at night with a torch, and pick off any slugs or snails you find. The small ones often do more damage than some of the monsters you find!

Greenfly and blackfly can appear in huge numbers on your beloved plants. In contained areas, you can simply remove them with your fingers or gently wash them off with a hose, taking care not to damage the plant underneath. Ladybirds and their larvae love to eat aphids— see page 102 for instructions on how to give ladybirds a home.

Try to provide appealing habitats for birds and insects in your garden. If you can encourage creatures such as birds and ladybirds in, they will soon keep the population under control. See page 110 for suggestions on how to plant for wildlife.

Keep your plants healthy and happy by giving them the conditions they like best.

Water plants regularly. Never allow your plants to become very dry or very wet or they will become stressed and be vulnerable to attack.

Provide barricades to keep your plants safe from crawling or flying insects; old net curtains stretched over wire loops or plumber's hose will keep cabbage whites away from lettuces and cabbages.

A criss-cross of string will keep pigeons and other birds from pulling up your newly planted seedlings (they can remove an entire row of new plants in a heartbreakingly short space of time).

Grow companion plants; tagetes (marigolds) and scented geraniums deter insects which find their host by scent and also discourages harmful, parasitic nematodes in the soil.

Grow decoy plants—nasturtiums will tempt caterpillars and butterflies away from your cabbages.

Onions, garlic and chives can confuse insects like carrot root fly that find their food by smell. Pot marigolds (calendula), rue and tansy are all beneficial for the same reason.

Pick off any yellowing, diseased or damaged leaves and fruit immediately and handpick any unfriendly insects you find.

There are a few fungicides and insecticides that are acceptable to organic gardeners. Remember, even if they are naturally derived they are still chemicals so use them very sparingly.

One of the best ways to avoid a problem with insects is to closely plant a good mixture of fruit, veg and flowers. This way there is no one overpowering scent to attract the bad bugs, and lots of variety to attract the good bugs.

CONTROLLING WEEDS

In gardens with bedding space, lawn or even paving, invasive weeds can be troublesome. Rather than treating them with chemical herbicides, which can also affect the plants you want to keep, look for other solutions. You can find a selection of edible weeds on page 88.

Cover areas dense with weeds with a layer of leaf mulch, bark chips, or even a black plastic bag. This will block out the light and suppress weeds.

Try loosening the soil with a hand fork or hoe, then pull the weeds out including their roots, rather than spraying with herbicide. This is particularly useful for seedlings, but is almost a waste of effort for tenacious weeds like dandelions. Consider whether the weeds are really causing problems; if they're just unattractive, try cutting them down to the ground regularly—this method can eventually kill the root system.

Remember not to put seeding weeds on the compost heap. The seeds are unlikely to be killed, so you could end up spreading a fresh layer of weeds all over your garden.

IDEAS FOR EDIBLES
FRUIT & VEG

To avoid the sun making your carrot tops green, keep them covered up with compost. For instructions on how to preserve your carrots through the winter months, see page 98.

CARROT BOX
SONIA UDDIN & LEAH ELSEY

Grow your own fresh baby carrots on your doorstep—literally!

INSTRUCTIONS

1. Go to your local street market and pick up a discarded wooden fruit box—the deeper the better.

2. Line the box with newspaper, making sure that the gaps in the sides are covered.

3. Fill the box with compost.

4. Sow the carrot seeds thinly in rows approximately 5 cm apart and lightly cover over with compost. The seeds should be planted at around 2 cm deep.

5. Water using a plastic bottle with holes punched in the lid during the early stages so that you don't over-water or disturb the seeds/seedlings.

6. Position the box indoors in a very sunny spot near a window. The seedlings will be spindly and weak if they don't have enough sunlight.

8. If your seedlings come up densely packed, pick out the weakest looking ones to give the strong plants more room to develop. 5 cm between each plant should be fine.

7. After six to eight weeks, when the danger of frost has passed, move the box outdoors.

8. Water regularly and evenly to ensure your carrots don't get woody and split.

WHAT YOU NEED
Wooden fruit box
Newspaper
Compost
Packet of carrot seeds

Sow seeds in spring for harvesting in summer
Harvestable in ten to 18 weeks

Spring onions can also be grown in a box using this method. Sow seeds in spring, and remove the smallest seedlings to leave the strongest ones at around 1 inch apart, to provide space for the roots to grow.

HIGHBUSH BLUEBERRIES

ELIZABETH MCCORQUODALE

Blueberries are so suited to growing in pots that there really is no excuse not to grow them. The show starts in spring with a display of sweetly scented little flowers, followed in summer by a continuous crop of delicious berries just bursting with antioxidants and vitamins. As it grows colder the leaves turn an autumnal red and the show doesn't stop until the leaves drop with the first really hard frosts. Then it starts all over again the following spring. Magic!

INSTRUCTIONS

1. Choose a pot about 40 cm wide and 50 cm deep and fill with a peat-free ericaceous compost and/or composted pine bark. Blueberries need acidic conditions so don't use garden soil.

2. Plant your blueberry in its new pot and water in with rainwater. Tap water is full of lime and isn't acceptable to blueberries except as a last resort. Keep your plant moist but not wet and allow the top 2.5 cm of soil to dry out between waterings.

3. Place your blueberry in full sun or partial shade. Feed with an organic plant food for acid-loving plants or a homemade liquid feed and the occasional addition of weak tea. Don't add wood ash or egg shells as this makes the soil limey.

4. Add a 5 cm layer of composted pine bark as a mulch each spring, and after the third year prune out some of the oldest and thickest branches. Thereafter continue to prune out a third of the old growth each spring.

All the currants—red, white and black—as well as the prickly old gooseberry, can be grown in pots. Unlike blueberries, currants and gooseberries require neutral soil, so use ordinary compost from your bin, mixed with some garden soil, or a bought multi-purpose, organic, peat-free compost.

WHAT YOU NEED

Large, deep pot
Compost
Blueberry bush
Composted pine bark
Liquid plant feed
Secateurs

Choose a self-fertile variety such as 'Goldtraube' if you only want to grow one bush. With most other varieties you will need two bushes which will fertilise each other.

Increase your stock of blueberry bushes to grow yourself or to give as living presents by taking hardwood cuttings in spring—see page 79. Don't forget to water your cuttings with rain water.

CARTOON CRESS

EMILY HILL & WILL GOULD

Perfect as a child's first foray into gardening, and makes an excellent gift.

INSTRUCTIONS

1. Recycle toilet roll tubes and cut them in half using a craft knife.

2. Wrap old newspaper comic strips around the toilet roll and fold in at the top and bottom.

3. Squash down one end from the inside with a blunt object to make a base.

4. Fill with soil or compost and sprinkle the surface with mustard and cress seeds, or other sprouting seeds or herbs.

5. Place on a windowsill in winter, or in a sheltered spot outside in summer.

6. Keep moist but not wet.

7. Cress will be fully grown within two weeks. Harvest weekly using a pair of scissors, and re-sow.

Mustard and cress is one of the best plants for introducing children to the joys of growing edible plants. It can be grown in a variety of containers, including an empty eggshell stuffed with a layer of wet cotton wool.

WHAT YOU NEED

Cardboard tubes
Craft knife
Decorative paper
Compost
Mustard and cress seeds

Sow indoors all year round
Harvest when leaves appear, after about a week

Other seeds to grow for green sprouts are corn, radish, peas, sunflowers, and broccoli, which is full of antioxidants and folic acid.

Always use organic seed for sprouting and seed which has been produced for human consumption rather than for animal or bird feed.

IDEAS FOR EDIBLES: FRUIT & VEG
CARTOON CRESS

GROWING STUFF
AN ALTERNATIVE GUIDE TO GARDENING

BEETROOT BOX

SONIA UDDIN & LEAH ELSEY

Try the beetroot cultivar 'Boltardy', which can be sown in early spring.

Beetroot grows well in deep containers—make room for the roots!

WHAT YOU NEED

Large container (at least 25 cm deep) —an old wine crate is ideal
Compost
Beetroot seeds

Sow seeds in spring
Harvestable in eight to 12 weeks

INSTRUCTIONS

1. Firstly, soak the number of seeds you want to sow in warm water for approximately one hour as the seeds are dry and quite tough—this will encourage quicker germination.

2. Fill a large container with compost and sow the beetroot seeds into the container 10–15 cm apart. Don't cramp them by sowing too close together, otherwise the developing roots will be restricted. Several seedlings will sprout from each 'seed' so sow them thinly and if cramped, thin them out when the seedlings first appear.

3. After the danger of frost has passed, place the container outdoors in a bright position to continue growing.

4. Keep the plants well watered to stop the roots from drying out. Remember, this is a root vegetable and moisture means tender and sweet-tasting vegetables.

5. Harvesting can take place after around three months, when the roots are around golf ball size. Harvest only a few at a time, leaving the others to grow on a little.

HOW TO USE

Baby beetroots boiled in their skins for 20 minutes and then peeled are a delight, either served warm on their own or cold, dressed with a sweet vinegar or a spoonful of sour cream.

Use raw young beets grated in salads.

Don't forget to use the leaves, which are delicious steamed and anointed with the tiniest knob of butter and grating of nutmeg.

During the seedling stage, watch out for predators such as birds. Use a small piece of netting to cover the plants, or cut off the top and bottom of a plastic water bottle—leaving the middle part—to form a tube that you can use to place over the growing plant.

MINI WINDOW GARDEN

EMILY HILL & WILL GOULD

Grow your own year-round sprouting salad snacks.

WHAT YOU NEED

Plastic bottle
Craft knife
Newspaper
Compost
Sprouting seeds

Plant indoors, all year round
Allow one to two weeks for seeds to sprout before harvesting

INSTRUCTIONS

1. Recycle a plastic container, for example a plastic bottle or food tray. If using a plastic bottle, carefully cut it in half lengthways using a craft knife.

2. Line with newspaper and/or a thin layer of compost or soil.

3. Sprinkle seeds in a 'garden' layout.

4. Water regularly.

5. Harvest and re-sow weekly.

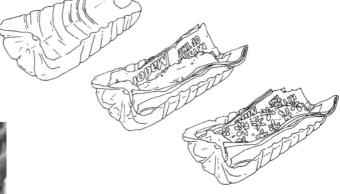

Sprouting seeds are widely available from health food shops—suitable ones include cress, alfalfa, mustard, lentils and quinoa.

TOMATOES
JOE HOLTAWAY

From seed to sandwich.

WHAT YOU NEED
Small pot
Compost
Tomato seeds
Small cane
Twine

INSTRUCTIONS

1. Fill a small plant pot with potting compost and place one tomato seed in the middle. Your seed should be approximately 2.5 cm below the surface of the soil. Water in gently.

2. As it starts to grow, give your tomato plant love and care. Tomatoes grow best in a warm spot, and need regular watering.

3. When the plant gets a little taller, put in a small cane to keep it standing upright. The cane can be replaced for a larger one as the plant continues to grow.

4. When your plant begins to outgrow its small cane it is time to think about the move outside; to allow your plant to acclimatise, take it outside for a couple of hours on a warm day, every day for a week or so. Your plant can then be transplanted outdoors in a warm, sunny spot.

5. When transplanting your plant outdoors, consider positioning the plant under a small overhanging ledge, tree branch or window: something that you can tie a length of cloth onto. This will give your plant something to climb up as it grows too big for the cane—but remember to keep your plants in the sun.

6, Keep watering and feeding and your tomatoes will grow.

7. When they are red, pick, and eat!

It is best to transplant your seedlings at least a week after the date of the last frost in your area.

Ensure your seedling pot has drainage holes in the base: too much moisture encourages disease.

TOMATO AND PARSLEY BREAD

235 ml crushed tomatoes
235 ml water
7 g yeast
60 ml vegetable oil
80 ml honey
35 g chopped parsley
820 g bread flour

1. Heat your tomatoes in 235 ml of water until they are warm to the touch. Pour the contents into a heat-proof bowl (preferably pre-heated using hot water, to aid yeast growth) and add yeast. Stir the mixture, then add chopped parsley, honey, and flour. Stir again.

2. Add oil to the mixture, fold in, and cover the bowl. Leave for ten minutes to allow the flour to absorb the liquid.

3. Knead the dough for 20 seconds, then cover and leave for ten minutes. Repeat this process another two times.

4. Roll out the dough on a floured surface and roll into your desired shape. Place into an oiled bread tin, cover with wet tea towel (this stops the dough drying out) and put on a warm radiator. When the dough has doubled in size, cut slits across the top of the loaf. The loaf will fall but that is ok—this actually allows the dough to rise in the oven. Bake in a preheated oven (as hot as possible) for 20 minutes, then reduce to 180C/350F for 15–20 minutes.

Check that your bread is cooked by putting a knife through the top to the bottom—if it comes out clean of dough you're done!

CARROT WELLIES
EMILY HILL & WILL GOULD

Ideal for making juices and fresh soups.

WHAT YOU NEED
An old wellington boot
Compost
Pebbles or gravel
Carrot seeds

Sow seeds in early spring for summertime harvesting

INSTRUCTIONS

1. Find a holey wellington boot or make drainage holes in the sole of an old boot.

2. Fill the 'foot' with a layer of pebbles or gravel.

3. Add soil or compost to 1 cm from the top of the boot.

4. Sprinkle 15 to 20 carrot seeds onto the surface, and water gently.

5. Place the boot in a sunny outdoor spot and water twice weekly.

6. Remove small seedlings leaving just five or six. These will mature to fully grown carrots.

7. Harvest when you can see the carrot's orange 'shoulders' above the soil surface.

Allow two months to harvest baby carrots, three to four months for prize specimens!

COURGETTES
ELIZABETH MCCORQUODALE

Keep on cropping! The more you pick, the more they grow.

Every garden or balcony should delight in the inclusion of at least one courgette plant. Choose one of the bright yellow varieties to brighten up a dull corner or go for one of the traditional green types. You can cook them so many different ways, and at so many stages, from flower through finger-sized to absolutely monstrous, that you really cannot do without the indispensable courgette.

WHAT YOU NEED
Small and large container
Compost
Courgette seeds
Plastic bottle
Craft knife
Liquid plant feed

INSTRUCTIONS

1. Plant one seed on its side, 5 cm deep in a small pot of good compost. Water in gently. Place your pot in a warm place, keeping the soil moist but not wet, and move the pot to a sunny windowsill as soon as the seedlings appear.

2. When your courgette has developed four true leaves and roots have begun to fill the pot, you can transplant it to its permanent home—a 30–40 cm pot or a corner of the garden. Courgettes will appreciate a rich compost to start them off.

3. Protect your plants from slugs by making a collar out of a plastic pot with the bottom cut away and sink it into the soil around your plant. Sprinkle sand, wood shavings or any other slug-deterring material both inside and outside of the collar as extra protection. You can't be too careful at this stage as slugs are rather partial to a succulent courgette stem.

4. Give your plant a weekly boost with homemade liquid feed or organic seaweed fertiliser and extra dressings of compost or well-rotted horse manure whenever you can throughout the season. Courgettes are very hungry, thirsty plants—in fact one of their favourite growing spots is right on top of a recently turned mature compost heap!

5. Sit back and watch them grow!

PUMPKINS AND SQUASH

Grow these hard-skinned relatives in exactly the same way as their courgette cousins. Although their leaves scramble over a large area, pumpkins and squash only need a moderate 40 cm pot in which to grow. The little green acorn squash, the orange butternut and the curious spaghetti squash are currently the most popular varieties but there are literally dozens to choose from. Everyone knows pumpkins as mammoth curiosities but they can also be grown as tasty little gems to be used in soups, stews, cakes and of course, the velvety and scrumptious pumpkin pie.

If you have kids and you want to try growing a mammoth marrow, grow an extra plant just for the purpose. If you leave one courgette to grow into a marrow, the plant will think its job is done and will stop producing any more. To make your marrow unique carve a message into the very top layer of skin when it is small—as the vegetable grows, so will the message, getting bigger and bigger as the summer goes by.

COURGETTE FUDGE CAKE WITH CHOCOLATE BUTTER-CREAM ICING

One of the best ways to use up the inevitable monster lurking under the leaves is to make this rich moist cake. It's no light-weight but it is utterly delicious and dangerously moreish.

FOR THE CAKE
90 g butter
1 cup granulated sugar
2 eggs
1 1/4 cups self-raising flour
1/3 cup cocoa powder
1/4 cup milk (only use all if batter needs it)
1 cup finely grated courgette

FOR THE ICING
2/3 cup icing sugar
60 g butter
2 tbsp cocoa powder
2 tsp milk
Boiling water

Grease and line the base of a 10 x 20 cm cake tin. Place the grated courgette in a colander to drip while you get on with the rest with the recipe. In a medium bowl cream the butter and sugar together until light and fluffy. Add one egg at a time and beat well after each. Sift the flour and cocoa powder into the bowl and stir in along with the grated courgettes. Add the milk a bit at a time until batter is pourable but not runny. Pour batter into prepared tin, place in an oven at 180C/350F for 45 minutes or until a knife pushed into the centre comes out clean. Cool in the tin.

To prepare the icing, mix cocoa with 1 or 2 teaspoons of boiling water until dissolved, allow to cool, then beat with remaining ingredients and spread on the cake.

GROWING STUFF
AN ALTERNATIVE GUIDE TO GARDENING

WINTER WINDOW BOX

EMILY HILL & WILL GOULD

Enjoy fresh greens throughout the autumn and winter months.

Although salad plants won't grow during winter, they will survive and can therefore provide you with fresh edibles even when it's cold. The more you plant during the summer, the larger your potential winter crop will be.

INSTRUCTIONS

1. Recycle an old drawer or wooden box. Drill drainage holes in the base or add a layer of pebbles or gravel.

2. Fill with soil or compost.

3. Sow seeds in rows approximately 5 cm apart. Leave intervals between sowings to produce a steady supply of greens and vegetables.

4. Water twice weekly.

5. Harvest as desired; they are great for salads and soups!

Hardy, easy to grow plants suitable for winter harvesting include chard, beetroot, shallots, and mizuna. Chard is easy to grow from seed and can tolerate shady spots and poor soil. Beetroot leaves are delicious and can be eaten in salads much like spinach, and shallots can be cultivated by burying whole bulbs just under the soil's surface. Mizuna is extremely hardy and will easily produce new growth when the weather warms up, ensuring an excellent supply of fresh leaves in spring.

WHAT YOU NEED

Wooden box
Compost
Salad seeds

RED HOT WINTER SOUP

4 beetroots
1 potato
2 carrots
1 shallot
2 pints vegetable stock
Salt and pepper
Tabasco sauce
Crème fraiche

1. Peel and grate the beetroots, potato, carrots, and shallot.

2. Put the vegetables together in a pan with 2 pints of vegetable stock, and season to taste with salt and pepper.

3. Bring to the boil then turn down the heat and simmer for 20 minutes.

4. Add a few drops of Tabasco sauce, a dollop of cream or crème fraiche, and garnish with a sprig of parsley.

AUBERGINE & PEPPERS

SONIA UDDIN & LEAH ELSEY

Using grow bags is a great, convenient way to grow veg in small spaces.

WHAT YOU NEED

Empty yoghurt pots
Compost
Aubergine/pepper seeds
Grow bag
Liquid plant feed
Canes
Twine

Harvestable in 16 to 18 weeks
Warm, humid conditions are best

INSTRUCTIONS

1. Make a few small holes in the base of some empty yoghurt pots. This will allow for drainage.

2. Fill the yoghurt pots with compost to just below the rim; this lets you water without losing the top layer of soil.

3. Choose which vegetable you want to grow and sow three seeds per yoghurt pot (although aubergine and pepper seeds are usually a safe bet for germination, a couple of extra seeds will be safer). Lightly water in.

4. Leave the yoghurt pots in a warm, sunny place indoors such as a windowsill.

5. When the plants have established themselves and stand at approximately 10 cm tall, you can plant them out directly into a grow bag. This can be done from late spring onwards.

6. A regular-sized grow bag will allow for two to three plants so cut equally-spaced squares (approximately 10 cm square) into the top of the bag, ready for planting into.

7. Regular watering is required for these thirsty plants, and liquid feeding is needed about once a week. To make sure you don't over-water, ensure that there are sufficient drainage holes in the base of

the grow bags, and only water when the top 3 cm of compost feels dry to touch.

If you have decided to grow both aubergine and peppers then it is best to keep them separate—plant them in different grow bags. Use canes to support the plants as they grow, using garden twine to secure them.

Once the vegetables start to appear, water and feed daily. You can make your own liquid plant feed, or use an organic tomato fertiliser—see page 106 for how to make your own.

Unless it's a very hot summer the sweet peppers may not change colour on the plant. In this case, pick them whilst still green and allow them to ripen in a warm room indoors to make red or yellow depending on your chosen variety.

If you end up with too many plants to fit comfortably in a grow bag, remember that these plants will be very happy in pots of about 5 litres (generally a diameter of about 23 cm).

Try using a polytunnel to give your veg protection from the cold—see page 100.

If your garden suffers from greenfly, try planting marigolds in the basket too as they are a great natural deterrent.

TOMATO HANGING BASKETS

CHLOE WELLS

There are many trailing varieties of tomatoes that need no pinching or pruning. They will all give you a super crop of tasty toms and look wonderful into the bargain!

INSTRUCTIONS

1. Sow seeds thinly in a container of moist compost, and place in a polythene bag in a warm area (an airing cupboard is ideal, but a warm, bright windowsill is also fine). Check daily and at the first sign of germination move the container to a well-lit, warm windowsill. Remove the cover.

2. Transplant the seedlings into individual pots, and when they have two sets of true leaves, transfer to larger containers 45 cm apart (you can normally fit three plants into a large hanging basket). This will ideally be in late spring/early summer.

3. Trailing varieties need little attention but are hungry and thirsty plants and you might want to mulch with comfrey leaves which are high in potash, or make your own liquid feed (rich compost is ideal but only feeds the leaves and not the fruit). Mulching around the base of the plants will also reduce water loss. You can experiment with lessening the watering when the fruits start to colour, as that is said to result in a better flavour.

4. Pick off any leaves that start to yellow.

5. Harvest fruit when evenly coloured. If there are any unripened fruit at the end of the season, place on a sunny windowsill or in a drawer with a ripe banana—just don't forget about them!

Enough tomatoes? Nasturtiums are very quick growing, colourful plants with edible, peppery leaves and flowers that look and taste great in salads. They are also a great one for kids to try growing, as the large seeds are easily handled; make sure you give nasturtiums very poor soil, or they will give you lots of leaves at the expense of flowers.

WHAT YOU NEED

Seed tray or other small container
Compost
Tomato plants or seeds
Hanging basket or other container
Canes
Liquid plant feed

STRAWBERRY BASKETS

Strawberries are another plant supremely suited to being grown in baskets, where they fruit away happily out of the reach of the dreaded slug.

Begin, as for tomatoes, with the biggest basket you can find, fill with compost and tuck five strawberry plants around the top. Feed with homemade liquid feed to encourage lots of flowers which will transform into lots of delightful fruit.

 Always add some sort of moisture-retaining substance to hanging baskets and smaller outdoor containers to prevent the compost from drying out. There are many kinds available but organic gardeners should look for one made from seaweed.

SUMMER RADISHES

SONIA UDDIN & LEAH ELSEY

Radishes are ideal for the amateur gardener and are also simple enough for a child to grow. They're quick-growing vegetables that grow extremely well in pots and are delicious in salads.

INSTRUCTIONS

1. Fill a large container with compost, scatter radish seeds very thinly (each radish needs space to develop) and then cover with a dusting of compost.

2. The container can be placed directly outdoors in late spring.

3. Once your radish seedlings develop, the plants will need very little attention. Simply continue to water them and watch them grow! If you give them the right conditions—good light and plenty of water, without letting them stay soggy—they will grow very quickly.

4. Radishes should be ready to harvest in about three to six weeks. Don't leave them in the soil much longer as they will lose flavour and crispness.

You can also grow the herb 'purslane', which is rich in Omega 3, in this way, as well as leafy lettuces like 'butterheads' and loose-leaf varieties such as 'Lollo Rosso'.

As they are so fast-growing, it is a good idea to plant radish seeds lightly but continuously, every three weeks over a number of months. This will provide you with a reliable, regular supply, rather than a glut.

WHAT YOU NEED

Large container (approx. depth 10 cm)
Compost
Radish seeds

Harvestable in three to six weeks
For summer varieties, sow seeds in spring
For winter varieties, sow seeds in mid-summer

SOY ROASTED RADISHES

Although delicious freshly picked or added to salads for a fiery kick, radishes are also lovely roasted to bring out some sweetness.

500 g radishes
3 tbsp peanut, grape seed or olive oil
2 tbsp soy sauce
Pepper

1. Remove the stems from the radishes, and cut the roots in half.

2. In a bowl, toss together the radish halves with the oil and soy sauce.

3. Add pepper to taste. Don't season with salt, as the soy sauce will provide this.

4. Scatter the radishes onto a baking tray, and cook in the oven for 30–45 minutes at 200C/400F turning occasionally.

A TREE TO TAKE WITH YOU

ELIZABETH MCCORQUODALE

We are a mobile society and it's not uncommon to move home several times. Planting a fruit tree in a pot means that wherever you go, as long as you have a little bit of outside space, you can have your very own orchard right on your doorstep.

WHAT YOU NEED

Large pot
Compost
Fruit tree
Liquid plant feed
Water absorbing granules
Mulch

Apples, pears, cherries and crab apples all have gorgeous blossom in the spring, followed by the thrill of the ripening fruit and often ending with a brilliant display of autumn colour.

You can choose a variety which has been grown on a dwarfing rootstock, a one year old maiden tree that's ready to be trained to any shape or, if you intend to grow it in a pot for two or three years and then plant it into a garden, perhaps you should opt for an ordinary medium-sized tree. This latter will cope with a pot for a while but will romp away when given more space to grow. Whichever size and shape you choose, you will also have the delicious dilemma of deciding which variety of fruit to choose.

INSTRUCTIONS

1. Find a large pot at least 40 cm wide and deep. If possible choose one that has a wide base, for stability.

2. Fill your container with a good, peat-free organic multi-purpose compost, and incorporate some kelp-based water absorbing granules (available from organic garden suppliers). This will make watering more satisfactory during the summer months.

3. Before planting, soak the tree in a bucket of water and then plant it to the same depth as it was in its nursery pot. Water thoroughly and apply a mulch to the surface of the compost to help retain moisture.

4. Feed your apple with a top dressing of fresh compost every spring and with liquid feed once a month throughout the growing season.

5. Prune according to how you want your tree to grow—as a minarette or column or as a standard tree. Ask for a demonstration at the nursery where you buy your tree.

How big will it grow? Choose a rootstock that will limit your tree to the size you want. This list is organised from smallest to biggest:

APPLES M27, M9, M26, MM106
PEARS Quince C, Quince A or EMH
PLUMS OR DAMSONS Pixy or St Julien A
CHERRIES Colt or Gisela 5
CRAB APPLES are often from a dwarf species although some will need the influence of an apple rootstock.

GROW YOUR OWN CHILLI JAM

NIKKI ARNOLD

There are over 200 varieties of chilli pepper in the world, each differing in size, shape, colour and flavour. Much easier to grow than you would think, they are a versatile cooking ingredient and can add a burst of fiery colour to your garden or home.

WHAT YOU NEED

2 small containers
2 pots
Compost
Chilli seeds of your choice
Cling film

Sow in early/late spring
Harvest in summer

INSTRUCTIONS

1. To start growing your own chilli plants you will need to fill two small containers such as yoghurt pots with compost—if your pots do not have any drainage holes, use a pen or pencil to pierce five or six holes in the base before filling. Tap each container gently to help the compost settle, water generously and then leave to drain.

2. Scatter approximately five or six seeds into each pot so that they are well spaced and lightly push the seeds into the surface of the compost using your finger. Cover the containers with cling film or a plastic bag secured with an elastic band and leave the seeds to grow on a sunny windowsill for approximately one week, until small green shoots start to appear.

3. Remove the cling film or bag and return the pot to the windowsill. Check the seedlings regularly to make sure that the soil has not dried out, and water them if they look a little dry.

4. Once the seedlings have grown to around 2 cm in height they can be separated into individual pots. To do this, fill slightly larger pots with compost and create a well in the centre using your finger. Gently lift out your chilli seedlings by the root ball and separate each seedling using your finger or a pencil. Drop your seedling into the well, pat the compost around the seedling to secure it in place and water. Keep your chilli plant somewhere warm and water regularly, moving the plant outside once the frost has passed.

5. You may need to relocate your plant into a slightly larger pot as it grows, and if it looks like it needs more support, push a garden cane into the compost and tie your plant to it using garden twine.

6. Use scissors or a sharp knife to harvest your chillies.

Remember to avoid contact with eyes and sensitive skin when handling chillies and to wash your hands thoroughly to avoid irritation.

You can keep chilli plants indoors, but they need a lot of light. If you can't give them enough light, outdoors or a window box is best.

TO MAKE CHILLI JAM

4–5 chillies (to taste), finely chopped
4 red peppers, deseeded and finely chopped
Fresh root ginger approximately 2.5 cm, finely chopped
200 g tinned chopped tomatoes
125 ml red wine vinegar
4 cloves of garlic, peeled and finely chopped
375 g caster sugar
Heavy-bottomed pan
Large spoon
2 small sterilised jam jars

1. Tip the ginger, chillies (with seeds), peppers and garlic into a heavy-bottomed pan and then add the tomatoes, sugar and vinegar. Bring to the boil and skim off any scum that comes to the surface using a spoon. When the mixture has come to the boil, turn the heat down to a simmer and cook for one hour, stirring occasionally.

2. At this stage, the jam should start to become sticky. If it has not, continue to cook the mixture until it has, otherwise your jam will not set properly.

3. Continue cooking for a further ten to 15 minutes making sure that you stir the mixture frequently so that it doesn't stick. It should now be thick and bubbling.

4. Turn the heat off. Allow the mixture to cool slightly before transferring the jam into sterilised jars, and then leave to cool completely before sealing.

RUNNER BEANS

SONIA UDDIN & LEAH ELSEY

Runner bean plants are excellent climbers! Try growing them up a drainpipe in a sunny position, or in a group of six or eight up a wigwam of canes in a flower bed. You can train them to grow up almost anything, and they are attractive ornamental climbers that will flower from mid-summer until the first frosts of autumn.

WHAT YOU NEED

Medium pot (diameter approx. 25–40 cm)
Compost
Runner bean seeds
Cane, 20 cm
Cane, 2 metres
Twine

Harvestable in 12 to 14 weeks
Sow indoors in mid-spring

You can also grow climbing french beans in this way, and Italian borlotti beans to be dried and eaten in winter.

INSTRUCTIONS

1. Fill a medium-sized pot with compost and sow one runner bean seed approximately 3 cm deep and water well.

2. Leave the pot in a warm, sunny place indoors such as a windowsill and keep the soil moist but not wet. After two weeks, a seedling will start to appear.

3. When the plant has emerged from the soil and at least four leaves appear, introduce a cane to provide support for the plant as it grows. When the plant is approaching the top of the cane, take the plant outside and put it in its final position. The runner bean plant will have naturally grown up the cane and spiralled around it. Gently unwind the plant from the top section of the cane and encourage the plant to start climbing a larger cane or drainpipe. As the plant grows taller you will need to use twine to secure the plant to the cane or drainpipe.

4. Runner beans need regular watering—in dry weather they will need a generous watering a couple of times a week; if they are allowed to dry out they will stop flowering, which will mean no more beans.

5. Once flowers start to appear, it will help to also feed your plants. Try making an organic nettle or comfrey fertiliser—see page 106.

6. Your beans should be harvestable from mid-summer onwards. Pick beans when they are still young and tender—about 15 cm long—as this will encourage a greater yield.

Try the variety 'Polestar', which will provide a reliable crop over a long season, and the beans themselves are stringless. Harvest them at 15–20 cm in size.

SUMMER SALAD
AIMEE SELBY

Lettuces are some of the most productive edible plants around. To save bedding space, or if you can only container garden, try this nifty idea for starting salad in plastic guttering.

INSTRUCTIONS

1. Cut a length of plastic guttering to size. Drill some holes along the bottom for drainage.

2. Fill the guttering with moist compost.

3. Sprinkle with a thin layer of lettuce seeds, and gently water them in.

4. Keep the guttering on a windowsill, in a sheltered spot in the garden, or in a cold-frame for germination—see page 108.

5. Seedlings should appear after a week, and can be planted out when the plants are around three weeks old. Dig a hole in the soil of a large pot or flower bed, and simply slide an individual seedling together with its soil, out of the guttering and into the prepared spot.

6. Refill the guttering with compost and begin the process again. By sowing seeds at three week intervals, you can ensure a steady supply of leaves and new plants until autumn.

WHAT YOU NEED

Plastic guttering, approx. 50 cm
Fine-toothed saw or hacksaw
Drill
Compost
Lettuce seeds

Sow in mid-spring to summer
Harvest throughout spring until early autumn

Try 'cut and come again' varieties of salad, which will allow you to regularly harvest the leaves, and your plant will happily grow more for you. You can sow seeds of this type densely, and directly into medium-sized containers. Harvest young leaves by snipping off the amount you need with a pair of scissors. Cut and come again greens include wild rocket, spinach, radish and types of lettuce, and seed mixes are widely available that will give you a great selection.

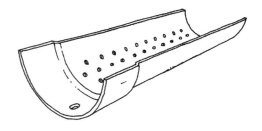

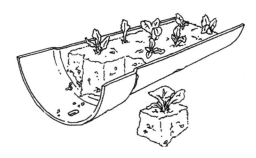

PEAS IN POTS
CHLOE WELLS

Peas are a great way of maximising yield in small spaces due to their vertical growth, and they're full of nutritious vitamins, especially when freshly picked from your own plant!

Collect the peas and store them in a clean, dry paper bag ready to be sown next spring.

WHAT YOU NEED

Container (terracotta will need more watering than plastic)
Compost
Pea seeds
Canes
Cane protector (plasticine is good)
Twine

Sow outdoors from mid-spring onwards

INSTRUCTIONS

1. Rich, warm compost is best. If it's cold outside, place your container filled with compost indoors for a few days before planting.

2. Make a 5 cm deep trench in the compost around the edge of the container, and plant two seeds at a time at regular 7 cm intervals. Cover with a layer of soil, firming gently.

3. When seedlings become large enough to handle, place a cane between each pair of seedlings. They may need to be tied gently until their tendrils form and guide the plant. Tie the canes together at the top with a piece of twine, and to protect your eyes, stick some plasticine or plastic bottle-tops on the exposed ends.

Watch out for strong winds as the plants act like a sail! Make sure your canes are firmly and deeply secured.

4. When your plant is ready to harvest, pinch out pods from the bottom to the top of plant. Harvest regularly to gain maximum freshness and nutrition, and make sure all pods are picked to extend the yield.

5. Peas can be frozen or eaten immediately—eat the pods too, which are crisp and tasty.

6. If your peas are growing in a bed, don't pull up the roots at the end of the season as there are valuable nitrogen-fixing bacteria here which are good for the nutrient levels in the soil.

7. If your peas are growing in pots the whole plant can be lifted and hung to dry, or just the remaining pods collected and left on a tray. When these pods burst of their own accord, collect the peas and store them in a clean, dry paper bag ready to be sown next spring.

To save space, peas can be propagated along a warm wall in a length of old guttering. Just make sure you drill holes in the bottom for drainage; the young plants can then be moved or transplanted without disturbing the roots, which they hate!

POTATOES IN A BAG

SONIA UDDIN & LEAH ELSEY

Here's a simple, space–saving method of growing your own spuds.

WHAT YOU NEED

Large brown paper sack (prettier than plastic)
Compost
Large polythene bag or heavy-duty bin liner
Seed potatoes

Harvestable in 12 weeks
Sow from spring onwards

INSTRUCTIONS

1. You can buy seed potatoes from a garden centre or try leaving your own potatoes from the supermarket to sprout green-purple shoots. The shoots should grow to about 2.5 cm long. You can do this by leaving them standing in an egg box in a cool place, out of direct sunlight. This head-start is called 'chitting' and can be done from early spring onwards.

2. When your potatoes have grown shoots you can start preparing the paper sack by lining it with a polythene liner. Make small holes in the bottom of the polythene to avoid excess water collecting.

3. Fill the polythene bag half-full of compost.

4. Plant the potatoes deep in the compost about half the way down. Plant around four potatoes, evenly spaced, per bag. They should be gently inserted into the soil with the shoots facing upwards.

5. When the new shoots grow to about 15–20 cm tall, cover them up again with more compost, taking care not to damage the leaves or stems. Continue to do this as the shoots grow until you have a full bag of compost—and potatoes!

6. Water the compost and place outdoors. Ensure you continue to water the plants regularly, or your yield will be low.

7. After six to eight weeks you can start searching your paper sack for new potatoes.

ROSEMARY AND GARLIC POTATOES

400 g new potatoes
75 g butter
2 sprigs rosemary
2 cloves garlic
Salt and pepper

1. Boil young potatoes for eight minutes, or until tender. Strain.

2. In a small pan, lightly fry finely chopped garlic in the butter.

3. Cover a baking tray with a large piece of tin foil. Lay the potatoes on the foil, and cut a 'cross' into the top of each potato.

4. Pour the melted butter and garlic over the potatoes.

5. Tear the leaves off the rosemary stems, and sprinkle them over the potatoes. Add a pinch of salt and pepper, and then loosely bring the sides of the tin foil together to form a parcel.

6. Cook in the oven for 45 minutes at 200C/400F.

An old compost bag turned inside out and with the edges rolled down is a good alternative container, as is anything of a similar shape and size that excludes the light. Try an old laundry basket lined with black polythene, a stack of old tyres, or a leaky water butt.

TALL TOMATOES
SONIA UDDIN & LEAH ELSEY

Tall varieties of tomatoes will really appreciate some shelter, and reward you with a better yield and longer growing season. Sonia Uddin and Leah Elsey suggest growing them in a lean-to shelter, which you can learn to make on page 103.

WHAT YOU NEED
A selection of small, medium and large containers
Compost
Tomato seeds—choose a cordon or tall bush variety
Canes
Twine
Liquid plant feed

Harvestable in 16 to 22 weeks
Sow seeds in early spring

INSTRUCTIONS

1. Sow your tomato seeds thinly in a shallow tray, water lightly and cover with a clear plastic lid (a used fruit punnet is ideal) or plastic bag. Leave the container in a warm, sunny place indoors such as a windowsill, but don't allow it to dry out.

2. When each seedling has two pairs of true leaves you can gently separate the seedlings and place them into larger individual containers such as yoghurt pots.

3. Once the tomato plants start to look strong and leafy, re-pot into the medium sized containers and add canes to support future growth. Tie the stems loosely to the canes using twine. Make sure you keep an eye on the twine so that as the plant grows, the twine doesn't restrict its growth or strangle the plant! Remember to keep adjusting the string.

4. When your plants start to look sturdy and the first flowers are showing, you can re-pot the plants into larger containers, such as supermarket mushroom boxes. Make sure you wash any container first using washing up liquid and rinse well so that plants aren't contaminated.

Tomatoes need warmth and lots of sun to ripen.

5. Line the tomato plants up against a wall and use a lean-to shelter to protect them. If your plants need extra support tie a long length of twine in front of the plants and across them to hold them nearer to the wall.

6. Water regularly and never allow the plants to dry out. If you have chosen a cordon variety you will need to prune the plants as they get bigger. Remove secondary shoots when they start to appear—between the stem and the branch—and pinch out young tips as they grow. You must prevent these shoots from taking nutrients away from the already established branches. Too many branches will delay the plant from producing flowers, and therefore tomatoes.

Liquid feed the tomato plants weekly during the flowering and fruiting period.

HERBS & FLOWERS

BOUNTIFUL BASIL

MADELEINE GIDDENS

Fresh, sweet-smelling and perfect for a sunny windowsill.

WHAT YOU NEED

Small/medium pots
Compost
Basil seeds

INSTRUCTIONS

Basil is a tender annual herb—it will die back once it has flowered and set seed—so you will need to sow a fresh batch of seeds each year. The most common variety used for cooking is sweet basil.

Sow straight into pots or plug trays from early spring onwards (aim for six to eight weeks before planting young plants outside, or if conditions are warm, sow directly outside but protect from slugs). Basil seed is very fine so you don't need to cover it with compost after sowing, just water in gently. They need heat to germinate so keep containers indoors if you live in a cool climate; alternatively place a plastic bag or recycled container over the pot until the seeds have germinated, then remove.

If there are any signs of 'damping off' disease where the plant starts to wilt and go brown on the stem, water with chamomile tea or use as a preventative measure when the seedlings first appear. Be careful not to over-water seedlings because they are more likely to rot if sitting in water. You can cover the seeds when they are first sown with a thin layer of vermiculite which absorbs water, thus keeping it away from the base of the plant stem which is prone to rotting.

Basil has a long taproot so seed trays are not suitable for sowing into; use pots or recycled containers with drainage holes. It also hates having wet roots so water it in the mornings or midday; this will also help to prevent 'damping off' and root rot.

Basil prefers a rich but well drained soil in a warm, sunny and sheltered area; it can be hard to grow it outside successfully as it is very tender—a warm windowsill is best. To transplant, dig a hole larger than the pot you have and transfer the whole pot contents as gently as possible to avoid disturbing the main taproot. Water in well.

Keep watering regularly during the summer; basil wilts very quickly if in full sun or very hot conditions.

If you use basil a lot it is worth sowing seeds every two to three weeks so you have a plant to harvest from all the time; just rotate your pots to give the ones you've used a rest—it will save you money on supermarket herb plants.

If the basil starts to get leggy it is likely that there isn't enough light in that windowsill.

HARVESTING

The leaves can be harvested once the plants are approximately 10–20 cm in height with about six pairs of leaves present; harvest the tops above this. Make sure you pinch any flower buds off to maintain bushy growth and stop the leaves losing their flavour.

Towards autumn you can let some of the plants flower and then collect the seeds to use the following spring.

PRESERVING BASIL

It is best to use basil fresh when the leaves are young; pick from the top of each stem to encourage further new growth.

Basil can be dried but it isn't very easy to do and it doesn't usually retain much flavour once dried.

A good way to keep your crop is to chop the basil leaves finely and mix with some olive oil, mix thoroughly, place in a zip lock bag or freezer proof container for adding to soups, casseroles, and stir fries through the winter months.

If you want to preserve the whole leaf, brush both sides with olive oil before freezing.

BASIL PESTO

Serves four to six people
Timeframe: approx. 15 to 20 minutes

100 g fresh basil
120 ml olive oil
Quarter of a cup pine nuts
2 large cloves of garlic, finely chopped
2 tbsp grated pecarino romano cheese
1/2 cup grated parmesan cheese
Salt and pepper to taste

Blend all ingredients except the oil in a food processor. When roughly chopped, start to gradually add the olive oil with the machine running. Push down the mixture as necessary then blend again. Season to taste and blend to the consistency that you like; add more oil if necessary.

Serve on grilled tomatoes, on top of baked potatoes or french bread, or use as a stuffing for meat—it goes well with chicken, mix into pasta dishes or add to green salads.

If you are not using it straight away, you can put it into a jar; to keep it fresh make sure you cover the top completely with a thin layer of olive oil and replace the layer each time you use some. It will keep in the refrigerator for between one and two months.

Lavender pillows make excellent clothes moth deterrents—put them in your wardrobe or chest of drawers for hole-free clothes!

LAVENDER PILLOWS

RICHARD REYNOLDS

GUERRILLA GARDENING

Guerrilla gardening is the illicit cultivation of someone else's land. Its origins can be traced back hundreds of years but in recent years it has become an increasingly popular public urban activity, one that is often nocturnal and usually on neglected land. Those who take part are driven to take risks and break laws by a great variety of motivations. Like most gardens, making the land more beautiful and more productive is usually central to the guerrilla gardener's aims, but so too may be the political gesture of seizing the land or the social benefits of gardening in shared space.

A garden that not only looks good and smells good but also provides something to take away and enjoy at home is perhaps the best of all gardens—one filled with lavender does just this. For three years the south London troops of GuerrillaGardening.org have made fragrant pillows from their garden of 200 lavender plants on Westminster Bridge Road. The pillows are screen printed with their year of vintage and sold to raise money for more guerrilla gardening .

INSTRUCTIONS

1. Choose the lavender. There are many different species and varieties with wide-ranging hues of foliage and flowers. The London guerrilla gardeners grow English lavender (Lavandula angustifolia) for its powerful fragrance. The foliage is grey-green and the flowers are grey-purple. It is a vigorous plant that spreads to about a metre wide and nearly the same tall.

2. Plant the clumps. Space them a little less than a metre apart. Lavender is happiest in a sunny location in well-drained soil and needs very little looking after.

WHAT YOU NEED

Lavender plants
Secateurs
2 pieces of light fabric, approx. 15 x 20 cm
Needle and thread

3. Cut the crop. The flowers will bloom in mid-summer on long stalks that shoot up fast from the dense round clump at the base. Cut off the flower heads down to the bottom of the stalk. You can harvest at the end of summer when the plants have faded and their best show is over, although the strongest fragrance is obtained by harvesting a little earlier before all the flowers have fully opened.

4. Dry the lavender. Hang small bundles indoors upside down or by spreading your harvest in loose piles on a towel laid across a horizontal surface. Over a few weeks the flowers will gradually drop off. Give the crop a good shake from time to time to speed this up.

5. Make the pillow. Sew together two rectangles of light cotton or linen fabric inside out, leaving a couple of centimetres along one seam unfinished so that you can fill the pillow. Turn out the pillowcase and use a paper funnel to pour in the dried lavender. Be prepared for some intoxicating soporific aromas! When it is stuffed to bursting, hand stitch the open seam... and take a nap.

Caring for your plant: Lavender is a hardy evergreen shrub that is happy to grow in poor soil conditions and is extremely tolerant to drought. They generally need very little water but will need more if grown in a container.

ROSEMARY
MADELEINE GIDDENS

Rosemary is one of the most useful herbs to have in your garden or in containers. It is perennial, evergreen and so can be harvested all year round in most climates. It has small pretty blue flowers in the winter and early spring which are also edible so they can be used in cooking.

WHAT YOU NEED
Pots or module trays
Compost/sand mix
Rosemary plant
Sharp knife or secateurs
Plastic bag
Rooting hormone (optional)

There are many varieties of rosemary including white, pink or purple flowering ones. The most common is *Rosmarinus officinalis* which has small pale blue flowers and is used medicinally and for cooking.

There is also a prostrate rosemary (*Rosmarinus officinalis 'Prostratus'*) which is ideal in rock gardens or any other free draining area where you would like some evergreen coverage.

Rosemary is best bought as a plant rather than started from seed or cutting, as it takes two to three years to get to a size from which you can start harvesting leaves.

However, if you want to have a go at growing your own, the best way is from a semi-hardwood cutting from an existing bush; either your own or a friend's. Rosemary can be grown from seed but you will have to wait a very long time to get a harvestable plant.

INSTRUCTIONS

The best time to take cuttings is in the morning during the spring or summer, before the sun has started to dry the plant out.

1. Find a healthy plant and cut a 7–15 cm stem just below a leaf bud where the stem is woodier and therefore more resistant to rot and also where there is more growth hormone. Alternatively, you can take a 'heel' cutting which is where you pull off a side shoot from the main stem, taking with it a 'heel' or small part of the wood. Try to choose non-flowering stems with lots of leaves. Side shoots root better than ones taken from the centre of the plant.

2. Place the cuttings into a plastic bag with a few drops of water until you are ready to plant them.

3. Fill your pots to just under the rim with compost mixed with a little sand. Wet the compost but don't waterlog it; rosemary dislikes waterlogged conditions.

4. Strip the leaves off the lower part of the stem and push the stem end into the compost around the edges of your pots. You can place three to five stems around the edge, depending on the pot size and how often you want to transplant to larger pots.

5. You need to check that no leaves are in or touching the soil once you've pushed the cutting down (they will rot), but you need some upper ones so that the plant keeps growing. Remove any flower buds if you have used a flowering stem.

6. Cover the pot with a clear plastic bag to retain moisture but ensure it isn't touching the plant. Keep the pot in the shade, spray each morning with a mister as necessary. Remove the cover as soon as you see new growth or if the plant or soil seems to be getting too damp.

7. When you see some new growth or if you can gently pull on a cutting and there is some resistance, then it has rooted and can be potted up or transferred to the garden.

Cuttings usually take between two to six weeks to root depending on the type of cutting, time of year and the conditions they are kept in.

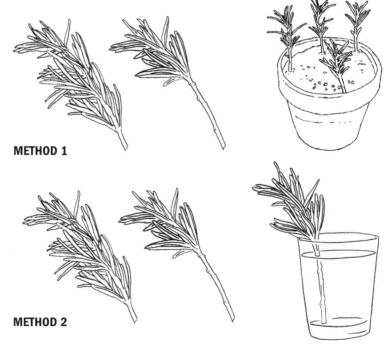

METHOD 1

METHOD 2

Another method is to root the rosemary in a container of water placed on a sunny windowsill—see previous page. Take the cutting as described above (heel cuttings work best) and just make sure none of the leaves are under water; this method can be quite successful in rooting rosemary within two to three weeks. You can then transplant carefully; make a large hole in the compost to accommodate the roots and part of the stem and place the plant in. Gently firm the compost back around the stem and water it in.

OTHER USES FOR ROSEMARY

· Make the woodier stems into rosemary skewers for the barbecue by stripping off the leaves and some of the bark and then soak in water before use.

· Rosemary leaves crushed with garlic and oil then mixed with potatoes that are to be roasted taste delicious (add in the second half of the cooking time).

· Make a rosemary syrup to serve with fruit salads, and to drizzle over sponge or lemon cake. Especially tasty with oranges.

· Make a marinade of garlic, oil, lemon and rosemary to rub into lamb or chicken.

PREFERRED CONDITIONS

Rosmary likes full sun and an open site with free draining soil. The one thing that will kill rosemary is if its roots are waterlogged. Make sure you plant in free-draining soil or place an inch or two of gravel in the base of the planting hole if you have very hard clay soil.

If you are growing in a container, make sure there is a drainage hole and that you use a free draining compost or mix in some vermiculite and perlite to aid drainage. Like most evergreens, rosemary won't 'tell' you it is unhappy due to too much or too little water until it is too late, so be vigilant!

WHERE TO PLANT

Rosemary is a very versatile plant. It is evergreen so it is great used as a screening plant; for example, use prostrate rosemary next to a manhole cover in the garden to cover it.

Upright varieties such as 'Miss Jessops' can be used to provide a short evergreen hedge, the height of which can be determined by how often you prune it.

Other 'woody' herbs such as lavender and sage can be grown in the same way as rosemary.

Rosemary hair rinse is great for dark hair. There are plenty of other plants that also work well—try chamomile for fair hair—see page 92.

ROSEMARY HAIR RINSE

Timeframe: Approx. 30 minutes excluding cooling time

Heat-proof container eg. jug
Handful of rosemary sprigs
Freshly boiled water
Vinegar (any type except malt)
Container for applying the rinse to your hair

This should give your hair a lovely shine and it also helps in stimulating hair growth.

1. Pick some sprigs of rosemary and place them into a heat-proof container.

2. Cover the rosemary with boiling water and allow to infuse for 20 minutes.

3. Strain out the herb and allow the liquid to cool to room temperature.

4. Add 1 tablespoon of vinegar and mix. Transfer, using a funnel if necessary, into a container that you can easily use to pour the mixture onto your hair.

5. Shampoo and condition hair as normal. Pour the rosemary infusion over your hair. Do not rinse out, dry as usual.

Mint likes to have 'wet feet' so it will fade and die in hot or dry conditions.

GROWING STUFF
AN ALTERNATIVE GUIDE TO GARDENING

WINDOWSILL MINT
EMILY HILL & WILL GOULD

For year-round mojitos and mint tea...

WHAT YOU NEED
Empty tin can or other container
Hammer and nail
Compost
Mint plant

INSTRUCTIONS

1. Wash out a used tin can and make drainage holes in the base with a nail and hammer.

2. Fill the can three quarters full with soil or compost.

3. Plant with mint cuttings from a friend or garden centre.

4. Place the can with a saucer under it on a windowsill and water it enough to keep it damp.

5. Harvest the newly grown leaves at the top of the plant for the best flavour and to promote bushy growth.

6. Pick a handful of leaves to make tea—see page 86.

Many of the mints that you can buy from garden centres or supermarkets are grown for ease rather than flavour. If you can find a really tasty plant in a friend's garden, then ask for some cuttings or even a clump. There will be a world of difference in the flavour.

Harvest the newly grown leaves for the best flavour and bushy growth.

Other windowsill herbs include parsley, chives, coriander and sorrel.

GROW YOUR OWN MOJITO

EMMA COOPER

There's nothing nicer on a hot summer's day than sitting outside and sipping a long, ice-cold drink. If it's cocktail time, then a mojito nicely fits the bill—and if you grow your own mint then it will be ultra-fresh and tasty.

Traditionally, mojitos are made with spearmint, a plant that is so easy to grow that it can get out of hand. It makes an ideal plant for a container, where it can be kept under control. It's not particularly fussy about the soil or compost that it grows in, and will cope with either a sunny or a shadier spot, and can even be grown on a windowsill.

WHAT YOU NEED

Medium pot
Compost
Spearmint plant

INSTRUCTIONS

1. Young spearmint plants are easy to find in the herb section at your local garden centre, and won't cost more than a couple of pounds. If you have a friend with a garden, they might have a spare plant to pass on.

2. Once you have your plant, you need somewhere to grow it. You could buy a plant pot, or recycle a container from around the house. Anything above 15 cm should be fine; you need something larger than the pot the plant came in, but not too big. The container needs drainage holes in the bottom, so punch some through if it didn't come with any.

3. Ease the spearmint plant out of its pot. Replant it in the larger pot, and add enough potting compost or soil so that there are no gaps and the plant is just below the top of the new container (this leaves some room for watering).

4. Give your spearmint plant a good drink, and leave it somewhere shady for a few days to settle in to its new home.

5. When the plant starts to grow new leaves, you can put it where you want it to grow. Mint is pretty hardy, but it will need watering in dry weather so keep an eye on it. The smaller the container, the more often you need to water. Placing a saucer underneath the pot helps to stop water draining away and keeps the plant happier for longer.

6. Harvest your mint leaves as and when you want them, all summer long. In the autumn you'll need to think about upgrading your spearmint into a larger pot, or dividing it—it doesn't like being cramped. Dividing mint is easy, and involves pulling the plant apart into chunks. Each chunk can be replanted to make a new plant, which you can keep or pass on to friends. You don't have to be gentle; mint roots are pretty tough.

7. Mint is a perennial herb and you can buy plants all year round. Outdoor plants die back over winter (unless you have a very sheltered spot for them) and grow new leaves in spring. If you bring a mint plant indoors over winter then you can have fresh leaves all year round.

MAKE A MOJITO

White rum
Lime juice
Mint sprigs
Ice cubes
Soda water
2 tbsp sugar

Mojito recipes vary, and no doubt you'll quickly come up with a favourite combination. For starters, try gently bruising 2 sprigs of mint to release the flavour, and add them to a glass with 2 tbsp sugar and the juice of half a lime. Add plenty of ice, a (generous) shot of white rum and top off with soda water.

Traditionally, mojitos are made with spearmint, a plant that is so easy to grow that it can get out of hand. It makes an ideal plant for a container, where it can be kept under control.

To ensure winter supplies of these herbal teas you can either bring a plant indoors in autumn, or dry sprigs of leaves (in an airy place, out of direct sunlight) whilst they are abundant in the summer months.

MOROCCAN MINT TEA

If hot drinks are more your thing, then growing your own is just as easy. Spearmint is used as the flavouring for the classic Moroccan mint tea.

Loose green tea
Spearmint sprigs
Sugar
Boiling water

1. To make your mint tea the Moroccan way, use loose leaved green tea and use a tea pot. Add 1 tbsp of tea leaves to a warm tea pot, and add a little bit of boiling water. The aim is to wet the leaves, and rinse them, not drown them. Tip out the water, leaving the tea in the pot.

2. Add a handful of spearmint leaves and plenty of sugar. Mint tea is served very sweet, so try 3 or 4 tsp or sugar lumps per cup.

3. Add 1 litre of boiling water and leave the tea to brew for five to ten minutes.

4. Serve the tea in small glasses, adding more sugar if necessary.

There are plenty more plants in the mint family that make lovely herbal teas, and many of them are just as easy to grow. A quick look around the garden centre should turn up peppermint, apple mint, chocolate mint and pineapple mint—all of which can be grown in the same way as spearmint. Some of the more unusual types are less cold tolerant, so check the label to see whether you should bring them indoors in the winter.

Another lovely herb to try is lemon balm, which is also in the mint family and grown the same way as spearmint. It's lemony instead of minty, and makes a very tasty and healthy herbal tea. It's great for soothing upset stomachs, sore throats and stuffy heads.

GROWING SUNFLOWERS

AIMEE SELBY

Sunflowers are one of the easiest plants to grow, and can be one of the most rewarding. They can grow to almost 2 metres tall, are bright and beautiful, and ideal for a child's garden. Not only will they brighten up your garden over the summer but they will attract birds and bees who love to eat the seeds.

WHAT YOU NEED

Small pot
Sunflower seeds
Cane
Twine

As the name suggests, sunflowers love direct sunlight
Sow in mid-spring to summer

INSTRUCTIONS

1. Sunflowers can be started indoors by planting one seed per small pot, at approximately 2.5 cm deep. Water the seed in, and cover with a clear plastic bag to keep moisture in. When leaves appear, plant the seedlings outside.

2. Try planting sunflowers directly into your garden soil—this can be done from mid-spring onwards. Sow the seeds about 1.5 cm under the surface, and make sure they get regular water. You can expect to see seedlings appear after three weeks.

3. Sunflowers are extremely fast-growing. You can expect to wait approximately two months until your sunflower is fully-grown and in flower. If you have chosen a tall-growing variety, you will probably need to tie your plant to a stake as it grows.

Planted in a row, tall sunflowers form an excellent temporary 'wall' to increase privacy in your garden—plant approximately 50 cm apart. There is also an excellent range of dwarf sunflowers out there which are suitable for growing in containers while still providing a splash of colour.

Sunflowers can grow up to 30 cm in a single day! Plant yours next to a fence or wall, and chart its growth.

EDIBLE WEEDS

EMMA COOPER & ELIZABETH MCCORQUODALE

The following edible 'weeds' are common, easily recognised and have been eagerly sought out in times past.

BRAMBLES

If your garden has been left untended for any length of time then you may well find that you have brambles—wild blackberries—taking over. Brambles are very strong-willed plants, spreading quickly by seeds dropped by birds and by long arching stems that can root wherever they touch the ground. They make a lovely wildlife habitat with lots of dense cover to hide small animals, and provide berries for the birds in late summer, but their thorns can make them unwelcome.

It will be down to pure luck whether the blackberries you find in your garden are tiny-fruited and sour or large and juicy—or anything in between—as there have been hundreds of different microspecies indentified.

To keep brambles under control you need to cut the arching stems down before they reach the ground, or pull them up once they have rooted. If you do choose to pull up your bramble stems, make sure you wear thick gardening gloves to protect from the sharp thorns. Established plants will have to be dug out. However, if you do keep your brambles, fresh blackberries are a real treat when eaten raw straight from the bush or cooked into pies and jams, made into blackberry vinegar or a delicious sorbet. You'll have to race the birds for your share, but a large bush will provide enough fruit for everyone.

DANDELIONS

Dandelions are not popular with gardeners. They have long taproots that are brittle and difficult to pull up. Any small sections of root left in the ground can grow into a new plant, so removing them completely is a time-consuming job. They also seed prolifically, so even if you remove all the dandelions in your garden, more are sure to blow in and grow next year.

The nice thing about dandelions is that they have edible leaves and are very hardy, so you can find fresh leaves in the garden for most of the year. Younger leaves will be less bitter and make a nice addition to a salad or a sandwich—the flowers can also be eaten in this way. The leaves can also be briefly cooked, much in the same way as spinach. You can even encourage the plants to grow milder, more tender leaves by blanching them. To do this, cover them with a bucket, or something to exclude the light, and the new leaves produced will be much paler and therefore sweeter.

Dandelion roots are also edible, so if you go to the trouble of digging them up you could try tucking in. They can be eaten cooked as a root vegetable, or roasted and ground into a coffee substitute for hot drinks.

NETTLES

People have been making use of the versatile nettle for thousands of years. In the past, nettles were so valued that when the Romans settled here they brought their own native nettle with them, only to find a slightly gentler species already in residence. Not only can they be used to make fibre for clothes, as herbal medicine and for fresh greens, but they are a valuable wildlife plant as well. They are a host plant for early aphids (greenfly)—which may not sound good, but means that any ladybirds that find their way into your garden will find something to eat and will stay to help you with your pest problems all summer.

Nettles can spread by seed and also by underground stems, so if you want to get rid of them you have to pull them up. But young nettle leaves, especially early in the season, are a very tasty vegetable. You'll need to wear gloves (rubber gloves are best) to harvest them, but once they've been even slightly cooked the sting disappears. The classic dish to make is nettle soup, but nettle leaves can also be treated like spinach or used to make a herbal tea.

Older leaves are not nice as they develop a gritty texture, but they make a great addition to the compost heap as they work as a compost activator, adding nutrients that encourage rapid composting. You can also use nettles to make an excellent home-grown liquid fertiliser—see page 106.

ELDER

The Elder generously offers us both flowers in spring and fruit in late summer and autumn. The flowers, sweet and delicate, can be dipped in a light batter and fried as fritters or turned into cordial, a light sparkling wine, or added to jams and jellies. The purple-black berries make one of the best hedgerow wines and, less well-known, a delicious autumn tart.

WILD STRAWBERRIES

The tiny berries of the wild strawberry, not uncommon as a garden weed, are sweet and delicate and though you would be extremely lucky to gather enough to feed a family, they make an exotic and delectable topping on sorbets and little meringues.

HAWTHORN

The very common hedgerow shrub and tree, the Hawthorn or May blossom, was well known to country children until recently as 'bread and cheese'. The young leaves and leaf buds have a mild nutty flavour, and children would pick them to eat as they played outdoors. We use them as additions to salads and, later in the year, use the berries to make wine and to help the set of other hedgerow jams.

SORREL

Common sorrel, with its lovely lemony flavour and Garlic Mustard (also known as Jack-by-the-hedge) are abundant and available all year round. Sorrel makes a beautiful and tangy green sauce for pasta and fish, while the smaller leaves of garlic mustard can be picked even in the dead of winter to add to salads.

You can also make use of the fruit of crab apples, rose hips, wild plums and wild cherries in jams, jellies, wines and autumn cordials.

Equip yourself with a really good book on wild food and go hunting—there's a veritable larder out there.

CHAMOMILE TEA

NIKKI ARNOLD

Chamomile is a traditional herb dating back to ancient times and is commonly used to make a tea from the daisy-like flowers it produces. Have a go at growing your own and then make a cup of this relaxing and calming tea.

WHAT YOU NEED

Small/medium pot
Compost
Chamomile seeds

INSTRUCTIONS

1. Choose a pot that has good drainage and fill almost to the top with compost. Lightly press four to five chamomile seeds into the surface of the compost so that they are evenly spaced and water generously.

2. Cover the top of the pot with a clear plastic bag and leave to grow on a sunny windowsill. When green shoots start to appear, remove the bag and return to the windowsill. Water the seedlings occasionally to ensure that the compost stays moist.

3. As your seedlings get bigger you will need to separate them into individual pots.

HOW TO MAKE HERBAL TEA

1. Place your chosen leaves or flowers (approximately five per cup) onto a piece of kitchen paper or towel and lightly crush them.

2. Put the crushed herbs into a cup or teapot, pour hot water over the mixture and cover. After five minutes strain the tea and serve, adding a little honey if you like your tea sweeter.

TO DRY CHAMOMILE FLOWERS

Drying chamomile flowers is a great way to preserve them for a stored supply of homemade tea.

Scatter the flowers thinly onto a layer of greaseproof paper on a baking tray, and bake in the oven on a very low heat (100C/212F). Keep the oven door slightly ajar to let the humidity out, and check

the flowers regularly to see if they're ready and to make sure they're not scorched. Turn regularly, and they will be ready in approximately four hours or when they crumble between your fingers.

Laying them on a rack or sheet in a warm, dark place works well too, such as an airing cupboard.

Why not try growing some of these other herbs using the method above—just remember to label each herb separately if you are growing more than one at a time.

Peppermint leaves make a calming and refreshing tea that can aid digestion and help settle the stomach.

Borage produces bright blue flowers that can be used to add colour and flavour to salads and summer drinks. The leaves can be used to make a soothing herbal tea.

Lemon balm leaves are particularly aromatic and make a refreshing tea said to soothe headaches and relieve tiredness—see page 86.

You can make a chamomile hair rinse for fair hair—see page 81.

MEDITERRANEAN WINDOWBOX

CHLOE WELLS

This windowbox is fantastic for those who want to garden but have no outdoor space. It will keep you in delicious herbs for much of the year.

INSTRUCTIONS

1. Line the bottom of your windowbox with gravel and fill with soil or low grade potting compost (you can mix a handful of gravel in with this too if you want). Place the windowbox in a sunny position, indoors or outdoors.

2. Scatter the seeds around the compost, water gently, and lightly cover the container with clear plastic or empty fruit punnets.

3. In small spaces pinch out overcrowded seedings, keeping the strongest. Transplant the others into smaller pots to give to friends or keep in case of disaster!

4. Prune plants hard after flowering by cutting them right back —alternatively prune them before they flower to keep a stronger taste in the leaves.

Purple sage is a good small variety for pots but likes wet weather even less than its common cousin.

Bay is good to grow indoors as it really dislikes the cold. Use a lot of grit in the compost and water very sparingly.

Other originally Mediterranean herbs to try include hyssop, feverfew, fennel, loveage and tarragon.

WHAT YOU NEED

Windowbox (with drainage holes)
Compost
4 handfuls of gravel
Sage, rosemary and lemon thyme seeds

FLAVOURED ICE CUBES

Freezing your freshly harvested herbs are a great way to preserve them for the weeks and months to follow.

1. Harvest your plant and chop into small bits using scissors.

2. Place the chopped herbs into the divisions of an ice cube tray and gently fill with water.

3. Freeze and remove as required for fresh herbs when cooking!

4. You can either defrost the cubes as you need them, or drop them straight into soups and stews for easy, home-grown flavour. Alternatively, try popping a couple of minty cubes into summer lemonades and drinks!

If you're planning an indoor window box, try some of these perennial herbs. They can be started at any time of the year—otherwise it needs to be frost-free and sunny for the seeds to germinate outside.

MINT FAMILY

These plants are very vigorous so they are best kept in pots rather than in gardens when they tend to take over.

Can easily be grown from seed or by transplanting roots. Once mint starts to flower, cut back (one branch at a time) for continually fresh, tasty leaves.

CHIVES

Grows easily from seed, each seedling producing a substantial plant within a few years. For prolonged use as a herb, cut the plant back to the base just after flowering, which can usually be done up to four times before it sets to seed.

PARSLEY

Plant seeds three months in advance of harvest. Requires warm soil and a sunny spot.

Cut half the plant back to near the base before it goes to seed, and the other half when you have fresh shoots, to ensure a continual supply of parsley!

Too many seeds? Throw them over some local waste ground or swap them with friends.

WILDLIFE
& PRACTICAL
PROJECTS

DIY ROOT CELLARING

RIVA SOUCIE

Riva Soucie grew up in a farmhouse with a delightfully creepy root cellar, perfect for packing away bushels of Yukon Golds, Cortland apples, bunches of fat carrots and low-hanging bags of onions. But even if you don't have a cold-floor basement with dirt walls, you can still store fresh produce over the winter.

YOUR MAKESHIFT CELLAR NEEDS
To be cool (or preferably, cold)
To be relatively dry
To be dark

Heat, moisture, and light are the enemies of proper food storage. Always keep your stuff cold, dry, and in the dark. If your building has no available cellar or underground storage space, look around for a suitable space under a stairwell, or in a cool corner of the laundry room. Similarly, if you live in a house, try an unheated garage, furnace room, basement, or shed.

You want the temperature in the space to be above freezing, but it doesn't need to be much colder than a refrigerator. Some moisture in the room where you're storing your produce is fine, and it is probably inevitable since cool places tend to be a little damp. Basically, you want to be sure to keep the goods from getting wet.

Certain foods store better than others. When in doubt, fill your root cellar with root vegetables. Anything that grows underground will store well underground (or in a cold place).

Potatoes need plenty of air circulation. Keep them loosely packed in a wooden or cardboard box. If the box is airtight, poke or drill a couple holes in the side or top. They also should be almost completely in the dark. Cover them with a few layers of newspaper before closing the box. You'll need to move them around probably once a week to once a month, depending on your storage conditions. Just stir them up a little, turn a couple over, shake the dirt out of the box, and replace the newspaper with fresh sheets. You'll soon be able to tell how often you need to tend to them by monitoring their rate of decay (i.e., softening, puckering, sprouting,

bad spots, and strange smells). Stored like this, potatoes will keep for at least four months.

Carrots also store very well, but there is a bit of a trick that will help them from drying out or going rubbery. Again, get a large wooden or cardboard box, but this time, line it with newspaper and then fill it part way up with sand. (Note: Try to make your carrot box inaccessible to cats, as they sometimes think it is a litter tray!) Then, just poke your carrots into the sand one by one (some can be touching) and cover them up. Like the potatoes, you should check them out every so often, but they're less likely to rot or sprout, and will keep for several weeks to a couple of months.

Onions store best off the ground. That means you want somewhere to hang them. Put them in a loose mesh bag or tie them in a large square of cheesecloth. Hang the bag from a nail in your root cellar or even in your pantry. They'll keep longer in the dark. Whole garlic bulbs also last a really long time if you stick them in a paper bag and keep them dry and in the dark.

Apples break down relatively easy if they are not properly stored. If you're just beginning or don't have access to the best storage, you might want to stick to McIntosh, Granny Smith, or other firm, sour varieties, which are less susceptible to decay. With the right conditions you can store even varieties with soft, sugary flesh. They should be loosely packed in a box (cardboard or wooden) that has a lot of air circulation. The apples should be dry and clean, as dirt on the surface of the skin promotes rot. Your apples should keep for at least two months when stored in this way.

The very easiest way to make a rough-and-ready root cellar is just to tuck your potatoes, onions, or apples into a paper bag or cardboard box before putting them in the pantry. This keeps them dry and away from light. They'll keep longer and be fresher, crisper and juicer when you use them. Check on your veggies every couple of weeks and always, always get rid of rotten produce immediately. You know what they say about bad apples....

Potatoes also store extremely well if loosely packed into the crisper compartment of your refrigerator.

MINI POLYTUNNEL

SONIA UDDIN & LEAH ELSEY

Great for grow bags!

If you lack windowsill space, you can make a mini polytunnel to keep your seedlings and plants in a protective outdoor environment, allowing the sunlight in and keeping the frost out!

WHAT YOU NEED

Wooden pallet
3 plastic hula-hoops or lengths of plumber's pipe
Wire coat hangers
Pliers
Hacksaw
Drill
Polythene sheeting

INSTRUCTIONS

1. Find a wooden pallet. Try a skip, or ask at a local construction site—builders' merchants are often pleased to get rid of their surplus pallets.

2. Find some plastic hula-hoops. You could try asking at a primary school having a clear-out; alternatively they are available cheaply at toy shops. Lengths of flexible plumbing pipe would also work well.

3. Using a hacksaw, cut through the hula-hoop in one place to allow it to spring open, creating a single length of tubing. Repeat with the other two hoops.

4. Find a drill bit the same diameter as the tubing so that it will fit snugly when inserted into the pallet.

5. Using the drill, make three evenly spaced holes in the top surface of your pallet, along the length of one side. Repeat on the other side, opposite the first set to create pairs of holes. These will allow the tubing to be inserted and held secure.

6. Now you can insert the tubing, creating three arches which will form the skeleton of the polytunnel.

7. Using pliers, straighten out the wire coat hangers. Secure these lengths of wire between each arch by twisting the ends around the plastic tubing—this will provide added support for the polythene sheeting.

8. Now you are ready to enclose the frame using the polythene sheeting. Ensure you leave enough excess sheeting that you can tuck it under the pallet at the sides to hold it secure.

9. Add a grow bag to grow vegetables inside your polytunnel.

Try growing aubergines and peppers in your polytunnel—see page 52.

LADYBIRD HOUSE

KATHY MARSHALL & JACK TOWNEND

This bug box will be used by ladybirds and other insects in winter.

WHAT YOU NEED

A piece of plywood
Logs (use sawn wood if logs aren't available)
Bamboo canes
Small sticks
Screws
Small nails
Wire
Power drill
Hand saw

INSTRUCTIONS

1. To make the frame, screw or wire together the logs.

2. Using a saw, cut the plywood to the shape of the frame and nail it to the back.

3. Cut the bamboo canes into short pieces, the same depth as the frame.

4. Cut pieces of log the same depth as the frame. Use a drill to make holes around 5 mm in diameter in them.

5. Stack the bamboo and log pieces into the frame. Push them in as tightly as possible so that they don't fall out.

6. Fill in any gaps with small sticks or moss.

7. Make a loop from wire to hang it from.

8. Hang your finished ladybird house on a wall, ideally facing into the morning sun. Position it near plants, as ladybirds like to eat aphids. If it is positioned low down and near a pond it may also provide shelter for dragonflies and solitary bees.

LEAN-TO SHELTER

SONIA UDDIN & LEAH ELSEY

Make a lean-to shelter for growing larger outdoor plants. The covered roof provides protection and the open sides allow you access to the plants for feeding and watering.

INSTRUCTIONS

1. It would be advisable to build your lean-to in an already relatively sheltered area, and use thick, sturdy lengths of wood.

2. Collect some wooden frames. You can use salvaged wood or to make a smaller version of this lean-to design, try looking in a charity shop for old picture fames.

3. Screw together three equal sized frames to make one large rectangle which will become the roof of the shelter.

4. Screw together two equal sized frames which will become the front supports for the structure. You may also want to add diagonal 'braces' in the corners, for further strength.

5. Using a masonary drill, screw a timber baton horizontally to the wall at your desired height. This is where the roof will be secured to the wall. Use L-shaped joist-hanging brackets for strength.

6. Using a step ladder, lay the polythene sheeting across the roof panels and use the staple gun to fix it to the frames.

7. Nail some thinner wooden batons over the edges of the polythene sheeting where you have stapled it, to re-enforce the polythene.

8. With extra timber, you can add extra struts to strengthen the sides of the structure.

WHAT YOU NEED

Timber frames
Heavy-duty staple gun
Saw
Drill and masonry drill bit
Step ladder
Hammer and nails
Large screws
Polythene sheeting
Joist-hanging brackets

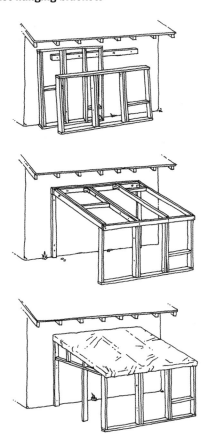

This is ideal for tall varieties of tomatoes —see page 70.

BUILD YOUR OWN WORM FARM

TRINA TUNE

Worm farms are a great way to convert food scraps into food for your garden and pot plants. By building your own farm, you also recycle many materials that would normally be thrown away.

INSTRUCTIONS

1. Choose your base box, which should be the sturdiest and most water-proof looking box. Punch a hole approximately 2.5 cm in diameter in one of its corners.

2. Cut the top off a bottle so that the part the lid screws on and its neck are still intact. Fit this through the hole so the bottle's opening sticks out the corner of the box—this must fit snugly. This will be the worm farm's tap.

3. Cut off the excess bottle, leaving about 2 cm inside the box. Cut a few evenly spaced slits into the extra plastic. Bend and tape the plastic down so that it fits flat against the walls of the box and is water tight. Mould blue tack around the edges of the bottle neck on the outside of the box for extra water tightness.

4. Pierce the base of the other box with small skewer-sized holes about 1 cm apart.

5. Cover the base of this box with a fine non-degradable mesh like fly screen, and tape the edges of the screen to the bottom of the box. The holes allow liquid to drain out of the box, while the mesh helps prevent worms from falling through the holes.

6. Place a rock or brick in the base box. In case worms accidentally fall through the mesh, the rock provides a place for worms to wriggle onto to stop them from drowning.

7. Rest the pierced box on top of the base box. You may need to tape it down to keep it in place.

WHAT YOU NEED

Two watertight, durable boxes eg. polystyrofoam
A lid or anything that can be used as a lid
Small plastic bottle
Durable, wide, waterproof tape
Skewer or sharp object for piercing holes
Blue tack
Old jumper, hessian or piece of material to cover the worms
Shredded newspaper, old compost, leaves or soil
1,000–2,000 red or tiger compost worms
Food scraps

Worms will eat most of your organic kitchen food scraps; however, steer clear of garlic, chili, citrus fruit, onions, dairy, meat, seafood, bread, fat, bones and oily food. They will also eat crushed egg shells, paper, dry leaves and ripped up cardboard.

8. Add about a 10 cm layer of shredded newspaper, old compost, leaves or soil to upper box. This makes great bedding for your worms.

9. Carefully spread worms over the bedding. You can find worm suppliers in the backs of magazines dealing with gardening or small-holdings.

10. Feeding your worms. To begin with just add a small amount of food scraps to the bed. Give the worms more food when they have eaten most of their previous meal. As the worms begin to breed In good conditions worms will double in population every eight weeks—add more food. Worms have voracious appetites and can eat through their own weight in food every few days.

11. Cover the worms and bedding with an old jumper, newspaper or hessian—anything that will keep the worms in darkness but still let water through. Eventually this will need to be replaced because it will break down and be eaten by the worms.

12. Add the lid. This can be the lid of one of the polystyrofoam boxes or anything else that can be placed over the top of the top box to protect the worms and keep vermin from getting in—they will be attracted to the rotting food scraps. Again, punch the lid with small skewer sized holes about 1 cm apart. This will allow rainwater to penetrate the farm to keep worms nice and moist. A rock or brick on top of the lid will prevent vermin or pets from breaking into the farm.

13. To harvest the worm juice, undo the lid on the bottle to let it drain out. Alternatively, let it constantly dribble out; just make sure you have a container underneath the bottle opening to catch the liquid. To do this, the base of the farm needs to be on top of something else so the container can fit underneath. It also helps to place something under one end of the farm to give it a slight rise. This will encourage the juice to drain out of the base.

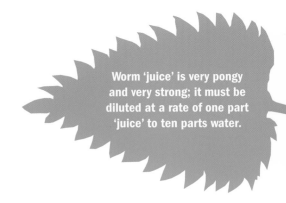

Worm 'juice' is very pongy and very strong; it must be diluted at a rate of one part 'juice' to ten parts water.

ORGANIC PLANT FEED

AIMEE SELBY

As spring gets into full swing, you might want to try feeding your veggies with home-made liquid fertiliser. It's easy to make, free, and will give your plants an extra boost.

Nettles make excellent plant feed as they are rich in nutrients. Best of all, it's a reason to control, rather than pull up, an invasive nettle patch in your garden. Comfrey and dock leaves are similarly effective, and can be used in the same way as nettles.

WHAT YOU NEED

Nettles
Gloves (rubber is best)
Secateurs
Bucket or similar container, with lid
Water
Weight (large stone or similar)

INSTRUCTIONS

1. Collect as many nettles as you can find. The younger stems are best, and this will also allow the plant to recover quickly, for your next harvest. Don't forget to wear gloves!

2. Using secateurs, roughly chop up your yield and put them in a bucket. Use a weight to hold the leaves down, and add just enough water to reach the top of the pile. Cover with a lid.

3. After around three weeks, your 'brew' should be about ready. Beware, as liquid nettle feed is rather smelly!

4. Your liquid nettle feed will be very concentrated, so apply it to your plants in a diluted ratio of one part feed, ten parts water. Mix this solution, and water your plants with it.

5. Rather than throwing the soaked leaves away, continue to add freshly collected ones to it, and more water as necessary. This will keep you in fresh fertiliser until autumn. When you're done, put the leftover mixture on the compost heap.

When harvesting nettles, take care to avoid harvesting ladybirds too! They love to live in these plants.

For acid-loving plants like blueberries, cranberries, camellias, rhododendrons and ferns (all of which are very happy to be grown in pots), you can save your coffee grounds, tea bags and tea leaves and add them to your nettle fed. This will make a brew that will acidify as well as feed the soil.

RAIN HARVESTING

SONIA UDDIN & LEAH ELSEY

You can make a simple rain harvesting system by collecting plastic drinks bottles—saving rainwater is a great environmentally-friendly and economical way of giving your plants a much needed drink, both indoors and out.

WHAT YOU NEED

Plastic bottles
Craft knife
Drill

INSTRUCTIONS

1. Collect some plastic drinks bottles, including one large water cooler sized bottle.

2. Use a drill bit the same diameter as the necks of the bottles to drill a hole into the base of each bottle—but don't drill the largest bottle as it needs to hold water!

3. Connect the bottles together by slotting the necks of the bottles into the holes in their bases. This will create a makeshift plastic guttering.

4. Connect the neck of the large bottle to the base of the 'guttering'. This bottle will serve as the main rainwater 'butt'.

5. Use the craft knife to cut one of the smaller bottles in half, across the bottle. Retain the top half and invert it, then insert it into the top end of the guttering. This will serve as a funnel for rainwater.

6. Install the water butt and guttering outdoors. If you have a shed or similar surface down which rainwater runs, it is best to position your rain harvester under this.

7. If there is no appropriate place from which you can collect rainwater run-off, try simply inverting a 'funnel' made from half a bottle (step 5) into a large water-cooler bottle, and position in a more open area of your outdoor space.

8. When enough rainwater has been collected, you can detach the large bottle and use it to water your plants.

This is especially useful if you're growing carnivorous plants, as on page 124, as they can only 'drink' rainwater, distilled water, or tap water that has been boiled and then cooled.

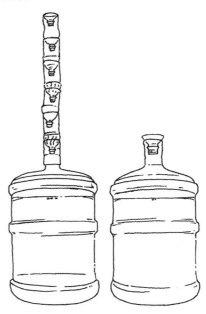

BUILD A COLD FRAME

HOAGY DUNNELL

Cold frames can provide a protective environment for vulnerable plants in the winter months and extend the seasons available to you for growing. Relying solely on warmth from the sun, a cold frame costs nothing to use and, by recycling old windows, very little to build.

Essentially a miniature greenhouse, the sloped glass roof of a cold frame provides a place to house your plants that admits sunlight during the day and reflects back some of the radiant heat which would otherwise escape at night. A frame will allow you to begin planting earlier in the spring and enable your plants to grow on later in the year, making it possible for hardy vegetables to yield an autumn and even winter harvest.

WHAT YOU NEED

Salvaged window(s)
Plywood sheet
Lengths of wood, 5 x 5 cm thick
Drill
Screws
Hinges

Your cold frame is also a great place to keep non-valuable gardening equipment and materials sheltered from the elements.

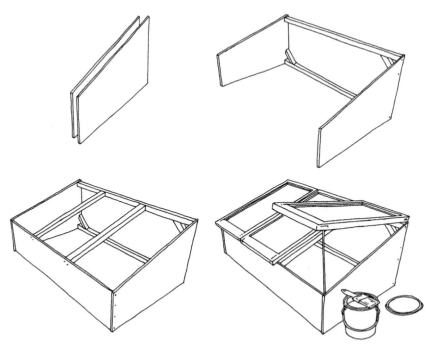

INSTRUCTIONS

1. Using plywood (preferably marine ply which is more durable but also more expensive), cut two sheets to roughly 40 cm high at the front and 65 cm at the back and with a diagonal slightly shorter than the length of your salvaged windows. These will form the sides of your cold frame.

2. Using lengths of wood 5 x 5 cm thick, cut two lengths a few centimetres longer than the combined widths of your windows. Attach these to the top and bottom of the back of your side panels. For additional stability add 45 degree braces at this point (if your cold frame is not going to be positioned against a wall you will need to use a solid back panel instead of struts, to compensate).

3. Cut and attach a strip of plywood the same length as your 5 x 5 cm wood across the front of the frame. Between this strip and the bar running across the top back, attach crosspieces positioned at the intervals of your window widths (hint: use one of your side panels as a template for the angles of your crosspieces).

4. Using hinges, fix two windows level with the sides and top of your frame, then space the others evenly in between leaving a small gap. The extra length of the windows produces a lip that will act as a handle and encourage water to run off.

5. For longevity, paint all exposed wood with a product intended for exterior use. For ease of use you may also want to attach supports to prop the windows open while you're working; these can also be used to prevent over heating on particularly sunny days.

6. All that's left is to position your cold frame. A shady spot won't provide enough heat so choose somewhere that receives ample sunlight throughout the day. Ideally, place your frame against the wall of a building which will further insulate your plants and allow them to receive some radiated heat.

PLANTS FOR WILDLIFE

EMMA COOPER

One of the great joys of gardening is being able to share your garden with the local wildlife, and to watch it come alive. It's certainly not hard to make your garden more wildlife friendly—birds and animals are just looking for somewhere to live and something to eat. Barren concrete won't entice them in, but adding a few plants will quickly get your garden noticed.

Lavender smells lovely and its beautiful purple flower spikes are irresistible to bees.

PLANTS TO ATTRACT BEES & BUTTERFLIES

Bees and butterflies want nice, open flowers that allow them access to nectar and pollen to feed on. Ideally, they want them for as much of the year as possible—right from when the days start to warm up until the first frosts.

There are plenty of plants that attract bees and butterflies, but if you're short on space then you might prefer dual-purpose plants that are useful to you as well.

The good news is that most herbs are great for both bees and butterflies. They have the right sort of flowers, and tend to flower over a long period of time, if you let them.

Anything in the mint family (including lemon balm) is good and will also provide you with a delicious harvest (see page 82).

Marigolds and calendula make great 'companion' plants for vegetables. Growing them near your veg will help to deter pests whilst attracting beneficial insects such as bees.

Marjoram and thyme are very useful in the kitchen and are excellent sources of nectar for insects.

More unusual herbs like Welsh onion and borage have truly beautiful flowers.

Early in the year, bees will love visiting the blossom on fruit trees and bushes, pollinating the flowers and ensuring a good crop of fruit.

PLANTS TO ATTRACT BIRDS

You might like to try growing a few sunflowers—bees love the big flowers, and birds love the seeds that follow.

Bushes that bear berries for birds include rowan, holly, elder, hawthorn, honeysuckle and ivy.

There are also some shrubs from further afield that are just as good—try cotoneaster, pyracantha and berberis.

Don't be too quick to tidy up the garden in the autumn. Faded blooms turn into seed heads, and food for the birds, and hollow stems provide shelter for beneficial insects like ladybirds.

Everyone loves watching birds as they flit around the garden. They really appreciate somewhere to perch, out of the reach of cats, so if you have trees or bushes in the garden then you're off to a head start. Even if you don't have room for a tree or a hedge, there might be one in a nearby garden that will do the job.

Different birds eat a range of different things. Some of them feed mainly on insects and will happily help you with your pest problems—snapping up aphids, caterpillars and other beasties as soon as they see them—others like berries or seeds.

If you put food out for the birds in the winter then try putting out different types of food, in different places, to entice in more bird species. Some birds are happy to eat on the wing, but others look for their food on the ground. A dish of water will be gratefully received on cold days when everything is frozen, and on very hot days in the summer.

If you or a neighbour have cats, you can still enjoy birds in your garden provided you follow a few simple rules: hang feeders very high up and in a spot where there is at least 3 metres of clear area with no cover for sneaky felines. Never provide nest boxes—newly fledged birds often hang around near their old nest, often at ground level, for several days before flying away. Bird baths, too, are out of the question; birds often become quite engrossed and forget to be wary when they're having a splash about.

To really encourage wildlife into your garden, you need to avoid using chemical pesticides and fertilisers. Not only do they kill beneficial insects as well as pests, but they upset the balance of life in the soil. A garden ecosystem is built from the ground up, with the beasties that live in the soil helping plants grow as well as being food for larger insects and small animals. The wildlife we love to watch—including birds, frogs and hedgehogs—depend on these insects for food. If there are no creepy crawlies then there will be no larger animals.

A great way to build up a healthy garden ecosystem and bring more wildlife into the garden is to make your own compost and use it to feed the garden soil. Many tiny animals at the bottom of the food chain live on decaying plant material, and find life very hard in gardens where all the rubbish is swept up and thrown away. Recycle all your garden waste via the compost heap, so that your garden can really come to life.

NIKI'S BIRD MIX

NICOLETTE MCKENZIE

Attracting wildlife is a valuable and enjoyable addition to any outdoor space. Birds will love this delicious and nutritious mixture of fruit and nuts!

INSTRUCTIONS

1. You can buy dripping cheaply from major supermarkets, or try collecting the fat from your dinner—collect from sausages, or roasting lamb or beef (never give chicken fat to birds). Put the fat into a saucepan and warm it though until melted.

2. Transfer the melted fat into your chosen container—be very careful as the fat will be hot.

3. Add the breadcrumbs (save your uneaten crusts in the freezer, then thaw and crumble), ends of cheese, dried fruit chopped apple and a handful of seeds or berries.

4. Stir the mixture together, and leave in the fridge to chill.

5. Transfer the container to the freezer.

6. Once the mixture has frozen, run cold water over the container to release the block of food.

7. Put in a hanging container for the birds to enjoy!

Try using different shaped containers as moulds depending on what shape or type of feeder you have, for example a small tin can for vertical cylindrical wire feeders.

Instead of fat to hold the seeds together, try using peanut butter, and hang it outside while still in its mould. Warm the peanut butter slightly to make it easier to work with.

WHAT YOU NEED

Heat-proof container, such as a used tin can
Small saucepan
Dripping or fat
Breadcrumbs
Dried fruit
Chopped apple
Bird seed or berries, or sunflower seeds from the garden

For use with empty wire bird feeders

SEED SAVING

AIMEE SELBY

As plant seeds ripen, why not take advantage of this excellent free resource and collect seeds for planting? Here are some ideas for annual flowering plants suitable for easy home-propagation.

TIME OF YEAR
Late summer to autumn

INSTRUCTIONS

Foxgloves, sunflowers, cosmos and hollyhocks are not only bright, beautiful and easy-to-grow plants, but they are all excellent sources of harvestable seeds.

1. When the seedpods and flower spikes on your plants look ready to split, snip them off whole using a pair of secateurs and place gently into a paper bag or large paper envelope.

2. Make sure you label the bag with the type of seed it contains, for later reference. Store the bag somewhere dry, and wait for the seeds to ripen—they will be fully ripe when the seedpods have opened to allow the seeds to be released.

3. On a clean surface, pour out the contents of the bag and separate the seeds from any pods or debris. Repackage the seeds in a paper envelope, seal, and keep them stored in a cool, dry place.

4. When it is time to plant your seeds, simply plant in a pot in a sheltered spot, or plant directly into the soil. The plants suggested here should be fine if used in this way.

Many other plants happily give up their seed, among them nasturtiums, runner beans, nigella (the little blue flowered love-in-the-mist) and poppies, as well as the herbs dill and caraway. Not all of them will grow up to be exactly like their parent plant, but they will all give you a speedy and trouble-free display.

You can also allow the seeds to fully ripen on the plant, but make sure you regularly check on them so that you don't miss your chance to collect the seeds.

CURIOSITIES
& OTHER THINGS

GROW A PEANUT PLANT

AIMEE SELBY

Peanuts grow on small plants that are really easy to grow yourself at home. They are fantastic as a child's gardening project, not least because of their unusual propagation method!

WHAT YOU NEED

Medium/large pot
Compost/sand mix
A raw peanut in its shell

INSTRUCTIONS

1. Peanut plants can be grown simply by planting a nut in the soil—you can use any unsalted, unroasted nut that you'd buy to eat. Peanuts with their shells are preferable as shelled ones can be dry—but you should still take the peanut out of its casing before planting. Plant one nut around 3 cm deep in a well-drained pot filled with sandy compost. Water in, and cover with a clear plastic bag to keep it warm and moist.

2. Unless the risk of frost has definitely passed, keep the pot indoors on a windowsill. Keep the soil moist but not wet, and a seedling should start to appear after only one week. You can put the pot outside in a warm, sunny spot, or plant the seedling into the soil once it is large enough.

3. As the peanut plant develops over the summer, it will put out clover-like leaves, and eventually yellow flowers.

4. It is fascinating to watch a peanut plant germinate. After flowering, the plant develops a stem that grows downwards and into the soil, and 'plants' a seed in the ground. This is why it is important to have a soft, sandy soil rather than clay, and a pot with a reasonable diameter.

5. If you maintain your plant properly, there is a chance that in the autumn, peanuts will be growing under the surface of the soil. You can feed these to the birds, eat them, or re-plant them!

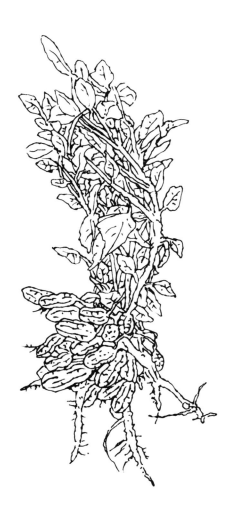

LIVING STONES
KATHY MARSHALL

Lithops, also known as living stones, are a type of succulent which have evolved to look like rocks to avoid being eaten in their natural environment.

WHAT YOU NEED

Bowl with drainage holes
Compost
Lithops plants
Grit
Stones or pebbles

INSTRUCTIONS

1. Select a bowl and fill it with gritty compost (about half grit, half compost). Punch through some drainage holes if the bowl doesn't have any.

2. Gently remove the lithops from their pots and decide where you want to position them. Carefully plant them in the bowl.

3. If required, fill in any gaps by adding more gritty compost, then cover with a layer of grit.

4. Place rocks on top on the grit. Try to choose ones that look like the plants.

5. Keep the bowl garden in a sunny position; it could be grown on a south-facing windowsill or in a greenhouse.

Lithops are very easy to look after. Each year the pair of leaves will split in half and a new pair of leaves will appear between them. When the old pair of leaves has fully died back, begin watering. Keep watering every two weeks until autumn arrives.

The best way to water your lithops is by standing the bowl garden in a saucer or tray and soaking the soil until water runs out the bottom of the bowl. Leave it standing in the tray of water for about an hour, then remove. Gauge how much water your plants need by only watering them if the compost is dry.

Lithops will flower every autumn. They produce yellow or white daisy-like flowers.

SEED BOMBS
RICHARD REYNOLDS

GUERRILLA GARDENING

Seed bombs are projectiles that contain the fundamental ingredients for a plant to grow—seeds, soil and water. They take inspiration from nature's naturally explosive seed sowing plants (watch out around a dwarf mistletoe in late summer) and from the destructive inventions of conventional warfare. Seed bombs are ideally suited for gardeners who want to grow things in places that are hard to cultivate such as behind impenetrable barriers or in places where spending time digging would be awkwardly time consuming. These convenient benefits make them ideally suited for inclusion in the arsenal of a gardener who has ambitions to cultivate beyond their own garden. Seed bombs can be made in the comfort and security of your own domestic munitions factory and the act of gardening is a fleeting moment of hopefulness. Unlike conventional explosives, the seed bomb will of course take weeks to germinate and still relies on the territory and surrounding conditions to create an impressive bloom.

INSTRUCTIONS

There are numerous different recipes for making seed bombs. The simplest (and my recommendation) is a mixture of wildflower seeds (native to your area), compost and clay dust combined in a ratio of 1:1:5 by volume and bound together with a splash of water. The clay dust is most easily obtained from a pottery supplier, many of whom sell large sacks of clay dust online, including exotic terracotta and local Devon clay. Roll the ingredients into projectiles the size of a golf ball and leave to dry out for a day or two. The seed bombs are now ready to throw onto your targeted territory.

Some people miss out the clay dust that binds the ingredients together and is nutrient enriching and instead use a capsule to contain the seeds and compost, such as empty eggshells and scrunched up tissue paper.

WHAT YOU NEED

Wildflower seeds
Compost
Clay dust
Water

CARNIVOROUS PLANTS

EMILY HILL & WILL GOULD

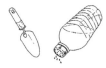

Natural pest control...

WHAT YOU NEED

Jam jar
Gravel or pebbles
Compost for carnivorous plants
Carnivorous plants
Rainwater

INSTRUCTIONS

1. No windowsill to hold your indoor potted plants? Be inventive: recycle jam jars, wire together and fix across your window frame.

2. Fill a jar with a layer of gravel or pebbles.

3. Add carnivorous plant compost (or a low nutrient alternative), until the jar is three quarters full. Plant fly traps such as venus flytraps, sundews and pitcher plants, and top up with compost.

4. Water sparingly with collected rainwater. Never let your carnivorous friends dry out, as they are bog plants and will die without water.

5. Many carnivorous plants die back during the winter and may appear dead for several weeks or even months.

JAM JAR CACTUS

NIKKI ARNOLD

Cacti thrive in hot climates and need little watering, making them one of the easiest houseplants to care for and a great project for children and beginners alike. They also look great around the home so why not give this funky jam jar idea a try, and see just how easy it is.

Keep an eye out for unusual stones, jars, coloured sands and different varieties of the cactus family to give a more individual touch to your project.

WHAT YOU NEED

Yoghurt pot
Jam jar or other glass jar
Sand
Compost
Cactus seeds
Stones or pebbles

INSTRUCTIONS

1. Begin by making several drainage holes in the bottom of a yoghurt pot. Fill the pot with compost and a generous pinch of sand. Mix well. Place the pot on a saucer to catch draining water.

2. Sprinkle four or five cactus seeds onto the compost so that they are well spaced and then water. Allow the water to drain out of the bottom of the pot, and then cover the pot with a small plastic bag, using an elastic band to secure it in place. Leave the seeds to grow somewhere warm, such as a sunny windowsill, until small green shoots start to appear. Be patient, this may take a few weeks.

3. Remove the plastic bag and then return the pot to the windowsill. Check the seedlings regularly but only water them if the compost has completely dried out. Once the seedlings have grown to around 2 cm in height they are ready to move to jam jars.

4. To prepare your jam jar, create a layer of stones and pebbles at the bottom of the jar and then cover with a layer of sand. Fill the rest of the jar with compost, which as before has been mixed with a generous pinch of sand, and make a well in the centre.

5. Carefully lift out a cacti seedling from the yoghurt pot and place the roots gently into the well that you have made in the jam jar. Pat the compost around the seedling with your fingers to seal any gaps and then cover any visible compost by arranging stones and sand over the top of the compost. Water your plant and position it somewhere warm in your home. Remember not to overwater your cacti, only water it when the compost has completely dried out.

FLOWERING TEACUPS

FLORENCE GEORGE

Why not make art happen in real life rather than keeping it within a gallery. Florence George attempts to create convivial opportunities in the public realm, in particular for people who wouldn't normally come across contemporary art in their everyday life. Here she shows you too can become a part of this fun, creative and rewarding project.

WHAT YOU NEED

Your choice of container—teacups, milk jugs, and sugar bowls work well
Small plant
Compost

Try using primroses in spring or winter-flowering pansies.

INSTRUCTIONS

1. Select your container—cups can be bought cheaply from car boot sales, charity shops, markets, etc..

2. Select your plants—the most suitable are small indoor plants such as African violets and Kalanchoe, succulents and cacti, or flowering bedding plants. Look for plants that are quite small and have some open flowers but also buds ready to open—that way the plants will continue to flower for a few weeks. Once they are in the cups, bedding plants should grow but develop fewer new buds than if they were planted outside.

Although they grow better outside, the plants will last for a few weeks in the cups as long as they aren't over-watered (or left to dry out) and they have plenty of light.

3. Prepare your plants for planting. Gently remove them from their pots and release the roots by lightly loosening the soil.

4. Place the plants in the cups, and fill in any gaps with extra compost as needed. Water gently.

5. The cups have no drainage so be careful not to over water. If the plants outgrow the cups, they can be re-potted into flower pots either in the house or in the garden if they are outdoor plants.

OPTIONAL

6. Choose your favourite inspirational phrase or saying, write the phrase on a tag or miniature 'flag' and attach to the cup.

7. Put the flag in the cup and leave in a public place for someone to find.

GARDEN IN A SUITCASE

SHARON BENNETT

Alpine plants and flowers are ideal for this project because they are small, hardy and easy to care for. You could try growing turf from seed; alternatively it is available from good garden centres. Bonsai trees or miniature topiary add interest; bedding plants and even vegetables or herbs are also possibilities providing they are relatively small and reasonably slow-growing.

WHAT YOU NEED

Suitcase	Pots for plants
Wood/plywood	Compost
Baton wood for legs,	Plastic lining
approximately 2.5 x 2.5 cm	Gravel
Wooden beading	String
Saw	Plants
Jigsaw	Miniature garden furniture
Screwdriver and screws	(optional)
PVA glue	

INSTRUCTIONS

1. Get an old suitcase.

2. Measure the wood to fit inside the case and cut to size using a saw.

3. Measure and cut four equal 'legs' to raise the wood to just below the depth of the suitcase and screw the legs to the wood. This creates a false bottom to the case with room underneath for the plant pots.

4. Choose plants to put in the garden.

5. Decide where the pots are going to go and cut holes in the wood for the plant pots using a small saw and a jigsaw.

6. If your garden is going to have a lawn, fill the pots with compost and lay the turf on top. Press down well.

7. Put lengths of beading around the edge of the wood—this is to stop the gravel falling over the edge and can be done using PVA glue.

8. Drill four holes in the wood—two evenly spaced on each short edge—and tie two string loops to create handles so that lifting the wood in and out of the suitcase is easier.

9. Line the suitcase with plastic sheeting. This is to catch any excess water after watering the plants.

10. Place the pots into the holes you have cut, and put a small layer of gravel in the bottom of each to help with drainage.

11. Put gravel around the pots to hide the wood and the edges of the pots. You can add miniature furniture or objects to your garden (optional) to create a feature.

12. You can give the plants a little water whilst in the case but periodically remove the gravel and take the pots out of the case to make watering and drainage easier. Remove any excess water from inside the case.

13. The lawn will grow, so trim regularly with scissors to keep it looking neat. Water regularly and keep in a place that has lots of light but isn't open to extreme temperatures.

RESOURCES

KEEPING YOUR GARDENING GREEN

ELIZABETH MCCORQUODALE

The worldwide gardening industry turns over billions of pounds each year, but because of its nature it has been regarded as one of the more benign forces in the big business world. However it doesn't take too much digging to reveal the less than green truth. Overall, the industry is a massive consumer of natural resources in the form of water, energy and raw materials. Plastic pots are used once and discarded. Peat and topsoil, to be used by growers and sold, bagged up, to the public, is scraped from the countryside— and not necessarily our countryside—without care or thought for the consequences. Chemical fertilisers and pesticides are used injudiciously to bring us the greenest, most alluring plant in the prettiest plastic pot—and we pay for the privilege.

Consider that same plant, raised by yourself from a seed or a cutting, and grown on your own windowsill in soil that you made yourself from kitchen scraps, in a pot that once held strawberries. Now take a snipping of the leaves and add them to your salad. You know where it's come from and you know what is in it; it really is satisfying.

Cutting out the big business, as far as possible, from your gardening venture really does make sound ecological and economical sense, and moreover, it's incredibly easy to do.

There is nothing to be gained—except uniformity—in parting with your hard-earned cash at the garden centre desk in exchange for a stack of containers, the like of which you have just dumped into your recycling bin in the form of yogurt pots and tin cans. Garden centres are now recycling plastic pots of all sizes, partly because of the backlash against an industry so contradictory in its reliance on questionable production practices versus its ostensibly 'green' image. Reusing these pots again (and again!) for their original purpose is commendable, and vastly more beneficial than recycling them. A trip to the supermarket will also net you an array of pots and seed trays in the form of mushroom boxes and apple crates.

Some local councils sell their shredded and composted material from the green waste section of the local tip and roadside collection. This has the great advantage of coming from a local source, so avoiding the pitfalls of long distance transportation. However, this compost may have been made from a variety of materials including lawn and garden waste which may have been treated with pesticides, and shredded timber which may include MDF, paint and other chemical treatments. Ask for the assurance that it has been composted to PAS 100 standards—the certification that guarantees that your compost has been made properly, is traceable and safe.

It can be difficult to find locally sourced, ethically harvested, clean soil (i.e. free of pesticides and other chemical residues). If you choose to go organic you're half way to ethical consumption because the ingredients are traceable and judged to be free of harmful chemical residues. Go one step further and always choose peat-free, especially those mixes that substitute by-products from other industries such as choir (coconut husks) and palm fibre (always choose one that is certified as having come from sustainable palm oil plantations).

In the end, the really realistic green route is to use as little bought compost as you can and supplement it with the stuff you make at home. You may have to make compromises—that's life—but be assured that growing stuff is a green alternative in itself.

CONTRIBUTORS

SHARON BENNETT

Having grown up in the Cotswolds, Sharon is always trying to find ways to bring the countryside into her urban life. She discovered her inner punk gardener as a child when she moved from painting faces on empty eggshells and growing mustard and cress 'hair', to using one of her mum's shoes to grow seeds in. Sharon has also started an office plant 'hospital' at work after discovering a worrying number of unloved ficus trees and yucca plants lurking behind colleagues' desks.

EMMA COOPER

Emma Cooper is a freelance writer living in Oxfordshire with her two pet chickens—Hen Solo and Princess Layer—and six compost bins. She's a plant geek who likes growing unusual vegetables; you can read her gardening blog and listen to her podcast 'The Alternative Kitchen Garden' at her website.
www.coopette.com

LEAH ELSEY & SONIA UDDIN

Leah Elsey and Sonia Uddin are artists who began working together after meeting at Central Saint Martin's College of Art in 2000. Their work aims to encourage dialogue and collaboration, which can inspire a cross-disciplinary approach and lead to exciting creative outcomes. In 2004 as part of their practice they set up a collaborative experiment to cultivate a variety of vegetables from seed in the courtyard at Chelsea College of Art. They continue to be inspired by open-spaces, monuments, social-sculpture and cultural diversity.

FLORENCE GEORGE

Florence currently doesn't have a garden and so looks for planting opportunities around the city of London. She thinks that it is important to take notice of and look after the world around us but believes that it is possible to make this fun and interesting rather than hard work. One of her favourite pastimes is scouring car boot sales and charity shops looking for objects that might come in useful one day. Her favourite city is Florence, of course, and she has a secret passion for musical theatre.

MADELEINE GIDDENS

Madeleine Giddens is a herb enthusiast who has studied herbs for the last eight years and focuses on sharing her passion of their gardening, cooking and craft uses via her website.
www.madaboutherbs.org

EMILY HILL & WILL GOULD

Emily Hill and Will Gould both live and work in East Kent; Emily is an artist and prop stylist, and Will is an artist and gardener. They met in 2007 through working in arts education and share a common interest in growing things. Combining their practice, the pair create 'living sculpture' that aims to walk a line between the man-made and the wild. Emily and Will are both members of St Duntan's Horticultural Society and can be found most weekends at Whitehall allotments, Canterbury.

JOE HOLTAWAY

Joe Holtaway was born by the sea in Cornwall, and currently lives in south-east London where he lives in a large vegetarian/vegan houseshare. He plays in a band, The Sea Kings and works a few days a week in a special needs school with wonderful bright children. He also loves to write and bake.

KATHY MARSHALL

Kathy Marshall is from Pudsey and has been interested in gardening since she was very young. She now grows a wide range of plants including cacti and succulents, caudiciforms, South African bulbs, orchids, ferns, gingers, woodland plants and aroids. Kathy set up the Herbs And Dragonflies group in March 2008 to encourage more people to love plants and the environment; they do craft and gardening activities with children, for free. She does voluntary work with other groups too and has planted up several beds of perennials around Pudsey. Her other interests are geology, painting and crafts such as mosaics, encaustic art and glass painting.
www.herbsanddragonflies.blogspot.com

ELIZABETH MCCORQUODALE

Elizabeth McCorquodale first studied horticulture and landscape design in Canada and, having spent several years in the garden retail and design sector, she quit the rat race and now spends her time growing stuff at her home in the Cotswolds. Her favourite occupations are working on her allotment alongside her husband and children, and going foraging for wild plants in the lanes around her home.

NICOLETTE MCKENZIE

Originally from New Zealand, Nicolette McKenzie has created at least two stunning small gardens in north-west London. A keen gardener, she is of the school 'why plant one when you can plant three...' and her gardens are full of birds all year round.

RICHARD REYNOLDS

Richard Reynolds is the author of *On Guerrilla Gardening* and runs www.GuerrillaGardening.org, the global online hub for guerrilla gardeners around the world. It is a place for people to find like-minded warriors, seek inspiration and share their successes and failures. It began in 2004 as a personal blog of Richard's solo guerrilla gardening in central London but has grown into a resource which links together guerrilla gardeners from around the world, whether they are lone activists or organised collectives with their own manifestos. Five years on GuerrillaGardening.org is still just a voluntary pursuit written and designed in Richard's spare time but is also a site with more than 100,000 visitors a month and many thousands of enlisted members.
www.guerrillagardening.org

RIVA SOUCIE

Riva Soucie co-edits New Social Inquiry (www.newsocialinquiry.com) and Supernaturale.com. She is a Registered Holistic Nutritionist, a PhD student, and a founding member of the Canadian Association for Food Studies.

JACK TOWNEND

Jack Townend is 15 years old and has had a keen interest in gardening and wildlife since he was very young, when he used to go on walks with his parents and grandparents in local woodland. Jack started to build bird boxes a couple of years ago and sold them to friends and family to encourage them to attract birds into their gardens. Last summer he made a ladybird house which proved to be popular with solitary bees as well as ladybirds.

TRINA TUNE

Trina Tune is a self-confessed composting and worm farming junkie with three compost bins and two worm farms in her backyard. When she's not busy composting, Trina works as a freelance writer and website content editor in Sydney. Her passion lies with gardening and sustainability. You can follow her journey in creating a greener, more sustainable life through her weblog.
www.greenfoot.com.au

CHLOE WELLS

Chloe Wells studied Fine Art at Reading University and graduated in June 2008. Her love of gardening started there and she created a garden on uni grounds. She has just finished an internship at Kew gardens and has her own gardening business. She hopes to travel to botanic gardens around the world.

GARDENING WEB DIRECTORY

USEFUL GARDENING WEBSITES

Royal Horticultural Society
Offering invaluable information on all aspects of gardening.
www.rhs.org.uk

BBC Gardening
A great website for beginners, offering manageable projects and step-by-step guides.
www.bbc.co.uk/gardening

Gardener's World
User-friendly guide to gardening projects of all sizes.
www.gardenersworld.com

Garden Organic
UK charity for organic gardening.
www.gardenorganic.org.uk

RSPB
With information on all aspects of bird watching, feeding and care, with an excellent a–z guide for attracting more wildlife to your garden.
www.rspb.org.uk

The Seed Site
Useful directory of everything you need to know about seeds.
www.theseedsite.co.uk

Soil Association
Find out about organic food and farming methods, with information on joining local sustainable food community groups.
www.soilassociation.org

Garden Organic
UK charity for organic gardening with advice on how to grow organically at home, and links to certified suppliers.
www.gardenorganic.org.uk

Life on the Balcony
"Gardening tips and tricks for apartment and condo dwellers", full of useful information on gardening in the smallest of spaces.
www.lifeonthebalcony.com

Gardening Tips'n'Ideas
www.gardeningtipsnideas.com

BLOGS

Concrete Gardening
"Urban gardening, without a garden."
www.concretegardening.wordpress.com

Garden Web
An international gardener's blog.
www.voices.gardenweb.com/garden_voices

Heavy Petal
One gardener's blog with an emphasis on growing to eat in small urban spaces; based in Vancouver, Canada.
www.heavypetal.ca

Cold Climate Gardening
Garden writer Kathy Purdy offers her advice on techniques and the hardiest plants for chilly climates.
www.coldclimategardening.com

GROWING YOUR OWN

Grow Your Own magazine
A great site for those wanting to nurture a successful kitchen garden.
www.growfruitandveg.co.uk

National Trust
Has a seasonal guide to what you should be doing in your garden, when.
www.nationaltrust.org.uk

Allotments-uk
The UK's largest online allotment community.
www.blogs.allotments-uk.com

National Vegetable Society
For the more experienced vegetable grower.
www.nvsuk.org.uk

Home Farmer
Online home of *Home Farmer* magazine, with a forum to discuss everything from foraging for wild food to rearing your own livestock.
www.homefarmer.org

SUPPLIERS

Crocus
Enormous selection of beautiful plants and gardening-related products for the beginner to the obsessive.
www.crocus.co.uk

The Organic Gardening Catalogue

All-organic seeds, fruit trees and vegetable plants, as well as fertilisers, feeds and soil improvers.

www.organiccatalogue.com

Thompson and Morgan

Every seed your heart desires.

www.thompson-morgan.com

The Organic Gardening Catalogue

Organic supplier recommended by the national charity for organic gardening.

www.organiccatalogue.com

Love Thy Space

Offers over 1,000 eco-friendly products for the garden and home including seed kits and biodegradable planting packs.

www.lovethyspace.co.uk

West Riding Organics Ltd.

Soil Association-certified composts and soil.

www.wrorganics.co.uk

The Natural Gardener

Fantastic site supplying natural weed controls, biodegradable containers and peat-free compost.

www.thenaturalgardener.co.uk

Wiggly Wigglers

UK supplier of home composting equipmment and composting worms as well as everything else you could need for your garden.

www.wigglywigglers.co.uk

City Farmer

A directory of compost worm suppliers across the world.

www.cityfarmer.org/wormsupl79.html

Mumm's Sprouting Seeds

Every variety of sprouting seed you could want, with comprehensive growing and nutrition information.

www.sprouting.com

Richters Herbs

Herb specialists selling certified organic and all-natural varieties, on the web and by mail-order.

www.richters.com

Suffolk Herbs

Online and catalogue shop for sprouting seeds, wildflower mixes, and every herb you could want.

www.suffolkherbs.com

Jekka's Herb Farm

Specialists in culinary and medicinal herbs, with advice on what to plant, when. Also runs open days and workshops at its herb farm.

www.jekkasherbfarm.com

COMMUNITIES

Seedy People

UK seed-swapping website.

www.seedypeople.co.uk/default.aspx

Seed Swap

USA seed-swapping community.

www.garden.org/seedswap

Freecycle

Fantastic resource to both offer and receive stuff for free—join the group relating to your local area and you'll find hundreds of perfectly useful bits for your garden, from tools to containers to plants, while keeping unwanted items out of landfill.

www.freecycle.org/groups

Guerrilla Gardening

Your first stop for guerrilla gardening information. Richard Reynolds' website charts the progress of the movement, with information on local digs, a community forum and great list of related links.

www.guerrillagardening.org

LA Guerrilla Gerdening

The site for the Los Angeles guerrilla gardening group, where you can find out about local digs.

www.laguerrillagardening.org

Green Guerillas

The group that originally coined the term 'guerrilla gardening' organise local community gardening projects for all ages and abilities and help sustain local green spaces in New York City.

www.greenguerillas.org

FURTHER READING

Bartholomew, Mel
Square-Foot Gardening: A New Way to Garden in Less Space with Less Work
Emmaus, PA: Rodale Press
2005

Boxer, Arabella, and Philippa Back
The Herb Book
Octopus/Mayflower
1991

Bridgewater, Alan, and Gill Bridgewater
The Self-Sufficiency Handbook
London: New Holland Publishers
2006

Caplin, James, and Adam Caplin
Urban Eden: Grow Delicious Fruit, Vegetables and Herbs in a Really Small Space
London: Kyle Cathie
2004

Davies, Jennifer
The Wartime Kitchen and Garden
London: BBC Books
1993

de Saulles, Denys
Home Grown
Boston: Houghton Mifflin Company
1988

Hessayon, Dr DG
The Fruit Expert
London: Expert Books/Transworld
1995

Hessayon, Dr DG
The Vegetable Expert
London: Expert Books/Transworld
1993

Klein, Carol, Michael Guerra, et al.
The Edible Container Garden: Fresh Food from Tiny Spaces
London: Gaia Books Ltd.
2005

Mabey, Richard
Flora Britannica Book of Wild Herbs
London: Chatto & Windus/Random House
1998

Mabey, Richard
Food for Free
London: Collins
1978

Paterson, Wilma
A Country Cup
London: Pelham Books Ltd.
1980

Phillips, Roger
Wild Flowers of Britain
London: Pan Macmillan
2001

Phillips, Roger
Wild Food
London: Pan Macmillan
1983

Reynolds, Richard
On Guerrilla Gardening: A Handbook for Gardening Without Boundaries
London: Bloomsbury Publishing
2008

Richardson, Rosamond
Food From Green Places
London: Weidenfeld & Nicolson/Orion Publishing
1997

Seymour, John
The New Complete Book of Self-Sufficiency
London: Dorling Kindersley
2002

PICTURE CREDITS

Vee Bee
p 124 (right)

Sharon Bennett
p 129 ©

Matt Bucknall
pp 11, 23, 71 ©

Colin Burke
p 120

Jason Burmeister
p 88

Erin Collins
p 40 (top)

Gemma Cox
pp 45, 54, 61 ©

Denis Defreyne
p 123

Nathalie Dulex
p 56

Hoagy Dunnell
p 108 ©

Rosie French
pp 14, 38, 39, 46, 47, 58
65, 69, 75 (right), 82, 83
85, 86, 94, 125, 126, 127
133 ©

Robyn Gallagher
p 87

Christian Gauthier
pp 27, 47 (top), 61, 63, 66

Madeleine Giddens
p 81 ©

Ali Graney
p 49 (bottom)

Thor Haley
p 80

Katie Hannan
p 118

Jens Hofman Hansen
p 123 (top)

Emily Hill & Will Gould
pp 38, 39, 49, 50 (top)
51, 124 (left) ©

Tony Hisgett
p 113

Gill Holgate
p 43

Gordon Joly
pp 41, 50

David Jones
p 53

Seong Duk Kim
p 93

Stefan Koelble
p 89

Anita Levesque
p 44

Anja Liebermann
p 112 (top)

Kathy Marshall
p 102 ©

Jon-Eric Melsæter
p 55

Kathryn Miller
pp 122, 123 (bottom) ©

Luke Miller
p 99 (bottom)

Irina Naumets
p 111

Amy Pearl
p 17

Bruce Peters
p 121 (top)

D Sharon Pruitt
p 105 ©

Richard Reynolds
pp 74, 75 ©

Christa Richert
p 95

Dan Shirley
p 79

Dani Simmonds
p 30 (bottom)

Juha Soininen
p 114

Stock Xchng
p 106

Stock Xchng
p 121 (bottom)

Viva Tung
p 28

Bill Tyne
p 112 (bottom)

Sonia Uddin & Leah Elsey
pp 34, 35, 40, 62, 68, 70
191 ©

Simon Wuyts
p 99 (top)

INDEX

The editor would like to thank all the contributors for their keen
interest, enthusiasm and generosity, without which this book would
not have been possible.

Thank you to Richard Reynolds for his time, and for wanting to
become involved in the project.

Thanks also to Nikos Kotsopoulos, Paul Sloman, Pernille Maria
Bärnheim, Nikki Arnold and Adam Salisbury for their texts and
picture research, and Rosie French, Matt Bucknall, Rachel Pfleger,
Live Molvær and Sarah Backhouse for their help and creativity in
taking photographs.

Special thanks to Elizabeth McCorquodale for her texts and
consultation, to Johanna Bonnevier for her thoughtful design and
dedication to the project, and Emily Breakell for her contributions
to the design.

Edited by Aimee Selby at Black Dog Publishing.
Designed by Johanna Bonnevier at Black Dog Publishing.
Illustrations by Hoagy Dunnell.

Black Dog Publishing Limited
10A Acton Street
London WC1X 9NG
info@blackdogonline.com

British Library Cataloguing-in-Publication Data. A CIP record for this
book is available from the British Library.

ISBN 978 1 906155 68 1

Black Dog Publishing Limited, London, UK, is an environmentally
responsible company. *Growing Stuff: An Alternative Guide to
Gardening* is printed on Zanders Matt, an FSC certified paper.

architecture art design
fashion history photography
theory and things

black dog
publishing

www.blackdogonline.com   london uk